Woodworking for Beginners

An Essential Guide to Learn All Secrets, Techniques and Skills of Woodworking with Incredible DIY Projects.

Roland Jackson

© **Copyright 2020 - All rights reserved.**

The content contained within this book may not be reproduced, duplicated or transmitted without direct written permission from the author or the publisher.

Under no circumstances will any blame or legal responsibility be held against the publisher, or author, for any damages, reparation, or monetary loss due to the information contained within this book. Either directly or indirectly.

Legal Notice:

This book is copyright protected. This book is only for personal use. You cannot amend, distribute, sell, use, quote or paraphrase any part, or the content within this book, without the consent of the author or publisher.

Disclaimer Notice:

Please note the information contained within this document is for educational and entertainment purposes only. All effort has been executed to present accurate, up to date, and reliable, complete information. No warranties of any kind are declared or implied. Readers acknowledge that the author is not engaging in the rendering of legal, financial, medical or professional advice. The content within this book has been derived from various sources. Please consult a licensed professional before attempting any techniques outlined in this book.

By reading this document, the reader agrees that under no circumstances is the author responsible for any losses, direct or indirect, which are incurred as a result of the use of information contained within this document, including, but not limited to, — errors, omissions, or inaccuracies.

Table of Contents

Introduction..**6**

Chapter One..**11**

Getting Started

- Gearing Up
- Deciding Where to Build
- What Projects Should You Start With?
- Getting the Proper Lighting for Your Workshop

Chapter Two..**24**

Wood and Your Essential Tools

- Hammer.
- Screwdrivers.
- Power Drill
- Saw, Hand
- Saw, Circular
- Saw, Jigsaw
- Tape Measure
- Chisel & Mallet
- Combination Square
- Clamps
- Sander
- All About Wood
- Ash
- Birch
- Cedar
- Cherry

- Fir
- Mahogany
- Maple
- Oak
- Pine
- Poplar
- Redwood
- Teak
- Walnut

Chapter Three..**49**

<u>Woodworking Techniques</u>

- Measuring Wood
- How to Cut Wood
- Drilling Holes Properly
- Understandings Nails, Screws and Bolt
- Gluing Together Wood
- Creating End Joints
- Properly Sanding Wood

Chapter Four **88**

<u>Storage Projects</u>

- Project #1: A Cabinet
- Project #2: A Workstation

Chapter Five 105
Indoor Projects

- Project #3: Floating Shelves
- Project #4: A Stool
- Project #5: A Pour-Over Coffee Maker

Chapter Six 123
Outdoor Projects

- Project #6: A Sack Toss Board
- Project #7: A Raised Garden Bed Planter
- Project #8: A Vertical Planter Stand

Chapter Seven 135
Applying Finishes

- Finishing Wood Dye
- French Polish Lacquer
- Oil Shellac Stain Varnish
- Water-Based

Conclusion 151

Introduction

Woodworking is one of those skills that can cost a bit of money to get started, since you need to get both tools and supplies. It quickly pays for itself with the amazing things you are able to create. In this book we are going to focus on making some of those amazing things. Not all of them, of course, since a book can only contain so many and the number of projects you can create through woodworking is only limited by your imagination.

If you apply your creativity to your woodworking then there is no limit to what you can create and the projects in this book have been chosen for both their practical value as well as their educational value.

First, it is important to take a moment to ensure that you have come to this book for the right reasons. Namely, that you aren't confusing woodworking with carpentry. This is a common mistake that beginners make so let us get it out of the way quickly.

Carpentry is the act of joining together pieces of wood in order to create structures. These are your houses, your apartments, your sheds and your barns. If you are looking to make a new barn for your backyard homestead or if you're looking to build your own house then you are going to want to find a book that is focused on carpentry. In this book our attention is on woodworking.

So what exactly is woodworking? Woodworking is the act of using our carpentry skills to create objects made from wood. The use of the term carpentry skill here is to let us know that woodworking still focuses on the joining together of different pieces of wood. The key point here, however, is that woodworking focuses on objects. From dinner tables to chairs, cabinets to standing closets, woodworking is all about these objects. They don't need to just be those found inside your house as these examples imply, though. They simply need to be made of wood.

In this book we're going to give our attention over to the various projects we can make. Before we dig into the projects we're going to take a few minutes to discuss Woodworking 101. We're going to briefly talk about how to get into woodworking, where we should be working our wood and what projects are perfect for beginners. This will make up our first chapter.

The second chapter will complete this section of the book by taking a quick look at the tools we use when working with wood. From simple handheld tools like hammers through to complex saws and planers, we'll cover not only these tools but we'll even take a quick look at the various kinds of wood we can use. If you thought all wood was the same then you're in for a shock!

With Chapter Three, we move into the second section of the book, the real meaty part which inspired me to write it in the first place. This chapter is entirely focused on the different techniques that we use when working with wood. These are important because they're what we'll be using as we move through the rest of the book.

Chapter Four brings us to the projects. Specifically, we'll be starting with a look at storage projects. You'll learn how to make your own workbench for your woodshop, plus how you can make a standing cabinet to store your tools, clothes or really anything you want.

Chapter Five then looks at indoor projects. These are things like chairs, tables, hanging shelves. Take a quick look around the room you're in and see how many objects you can spot that are made out of wood. Just around me I have bookshelves, the desk I'm writing at, a nightstand to hold up my fish tank and a barstool. Each of these could be considered an indoor project. How many did you find around you?

Chapter Six moves us outside. We can use our woodworking skills to build raised garden beds, sitting benches, garden trellises, birdhouses, picnic tables. The list is as long and varied as the list of indoor projects is, so much so that we'll only be able to look at a handful of the possibilities. To even try to curate a list of every possible outdoor project would be an overwhelming endeavor.

Finally, we reach Chapter Seven. In this final chapter, we'll look at how to apply a finish to our project. Considering that it comes at the end of the project, the term "finish" is rather appropriate and so it makes sense to close out the book with this discussion. For those that don't know, a finish is a stain, paint or lacquer coat which we use to really make our projects standout. A plain looking project becomes a masterpiece with the right finish.

So if you're excited to get building your own projects with your woodworking skills then you've come to the right place. What are you waiting for? Flip the page and dive in!

Chapter 1

Getting Started

Everybody has to start somewhere. Woodworkers need to start with preparing their working space and acquiring tools and this book needs to start with Chapter One. Why don't we combine the two together and spend this chapter getting our work space set up and prepared so we can get to the projects that much faster.

In this chapter, we'll look at how we acquire the gear we need to work with wood. From there, we'll discuss how we decide on a space to build in, how we properly light our chosen space and what projects are best for beginners.

Gearing Up

Gearing up is one of the funnest parts of learning any new skill. Who doesn't like getting their hands on some new toys to play with? It's like being a kid in the toy store all over again, only this time around it's a hardware store and it costs quite a bit more. I guess that's one of the few disappointments that comes with growing up.

The fact that it can cost an arm and a leg to get your woodshop up and running can't be ignored. This is a skill that can be incredibly expensive if you're not careful. Or, rather, it's expensive if you don't plan things out properly. I am a firm believer that planning makes all the difference, whether that means planning before a project or planning to make your own woodshop. If you plan out your purchases you'll find that they hurt your pocketbook far less while having the added benefit of not just sitting around and taking up space.

One of the big problems people face when they jump into gearing up without planning is that they purchase all sorts of gear that they don't need for the skill level they're working on. If you're at the stage where you're making birdhouses then you don't need a surface planer, there's just no point. You would be better served by spending that money on more wood so that you can keep practicing.

In the next chapter we'll be looking at the gear that we use when woodworking. This is the gear you'll be purchasing when you gear up your woodshop. Don't purchase everything in that chapter right away. Stick with the basics first. Make sure you have a hammer, some screwdrivers and a saw.

You could get by starting with a handsaw; I'd actually recommend getting a jigsaw, as they're incredibly useful even early on.

Give yourself a limit. Set down $200 to gear up and then don't go even a cent over. It's always tempting to purchase more, and it is especially easy to get upsold by a charismatic hardware store employee. By setting yourself a limit you'll get only those tools that are absolutely necessary.

If you aren't entirely sure this method will work then I invite you to take a look at the projects we're going to be working on in this book. You'll notice that even the coolest of projects can be made without expensive tools. Sure, those expensive tools will often speed up the process, but they aren't necessary.

With that said, if you absolutely must purchase a large tool off the bat (because you simply want to) then get yourself a table saw. It'll be the large tool that you use most often when working with wood.

Deciding Where to Build

It isn't enough for you to want to start woodworking and just buy some tools. There is still the big question of where you will work on the wood. You could purchase your gear and start working in the dining room on the table but this would get messy awfully quick and nobody would want to eat at that table again thanks to the mess. So it is important to pick an appropriate spot to work.

What makes a spot appropriate for woodworking?

There are three elements which you want to balance when picking a spot: Size, ventilation and electricity. There are other issues which you might want to consider, such as how hot or cold the space is and how much natural light spills into it; it is these three elements which you absolutely need to take into consideration when selecting a space for woodworking.

The first of these is space and it is also the most self-explanatory. If you don't have enough space in your woodshop then you won't be able to work on large projects. In fact, you won't be able to work on several of the projects in this book without a large enough space. When it comes to space it is easy to select a space which is too small but it is almost impossible to select one that is too large. So instead of worrying about what the perfect size is, instead it is easier to take a look at a handful of tools and figure out how much space they need.

If you are starting small, without purchasing any large tools, then you can get away with working in a much smaller space compared to what you'll need when you are working with many large tools. You should, at the bare minimum, select a space that has enough room for two work tables, a storage space for your wood and a table saw with two to three feet of clearance around it.

This should result in a space that is larger than you need when starting out but with enough space to grow it into a decent little woodshop. That said, it won't last forever. You will run out of space eventually with the purchase of additional equipment.

One other element of size that you should consider, though it isn't a necessity, is the size of the door to the woodshop. If you are looking to work on larger projects like tables, dressers, cabinets and the like then you'll need to consider how much room there is in the doorway. It's much easier to bring in planks of wood than it is to take out completed projects.

There is nothing more frustrating than finishing a beautiful project only to find that you have to take the door to the woodshop off its hinges to get it out. Okay, I lied. There is one thing more frustrating and that's not being able to get your project out of the room even when the door is off! You can avoid this frustrating experience by selecting a space with a large doorway, or at the least you should measure your doorway so that you know the maximum dimensions your projects can have.

After considerations of space come considerations of ventilation. This is a safety consideration first and foremost and one that you absolutely cannot skimp on. When working with wood, there is a lot of dust that gets kicked up into the air. These tiny wood particles can severely irritate your eyes, throat and lungs. I always recommend that people wear masks when they're cutting or sanding wood because this junk can often get knocked up into the air at the oddest times; sometimes, all it takes is a strong hammering. We can't expect to have a mask on during every step of the project, although

you absolutely should when sanding or sawing, as well as when you're applying a finish (as the fumes can be quite irritating and they're known to cause nausea).

By investing in some ventilation, you can keep the air in the woodshop clear. This is, by far, the best way to remove dust particles from the air so that you reduce the amount of irritation that you experience. It should be a no-brainer, because who wants to be irritated by their hobbies? Many people underestimate the value of good ventilation. I recommend that you purchase a mid-to-high range ventilation system and have it installed in your workshop. If this isn't possible then you may be able to make do with a window and a strong fan that can push the air out of the room. If all else falls, you always have the option of working outside, in which case you won't have to worry about ventilation as Mother Nature provides it for you free of charge.

Finally, the last key element you must consider when picking a space is the available electricity. When you are first starting out this isn't that big of a deal and that is why it is last on our list. When you have many pieces of equipment that eat up power, though, it starts to matter. The first thing I recommend, right out of the gate, is that you always turn off and unplug your equipment when you are done working with it. When something is plugged in, it eats up a small amount of electricity even if it is turned off and so unplugging helps to reduce the amount of electricity being wasted plus it also helps to reduce your power bill. The other reason to unplug your equipment is safety: you can't trip and accidentally turn on the table saw if it's been unplugged.

The best way to check the amount of electricity in your chosen space is to get a meter or a reader. Plug the reader into the outlet and see how much juice it has. Many readers allow you to plug a piece of equipment into it to see how much electricity it uses. This way you can see how much you have and get a sense of how much you'll use with each piece of equipment you've got. These numbers will serve you well as you continue to grow your woodshop.

Keep in mind that of the three key elements - space, ventilation and electricity - this third key is the easiest to fix since you can always use an extension cord to bring more power into the space.

If you keep these three elements in mind when selecting a space then you'll have yourself the perfect space for woodworking in no time.

What Projects Should You Start With?

When you are first getting into woodworking, it is unrealistic to immediately jump into making cabinets and dressers and desks. As wonderful and as fun as these are to make, they are large scale projects and this makes them a bad choice. It isn't that they are any more complicated than a smaller project: in fact, many large projects are easier to make than smaller projects; rather, they use more wood and so mistakes are more wasteful and costly.

In order to minimize the amount of waste we make when first starting out, it is best to begin with small projects. I recommend that you first make a shelf or a spice rack, something that you can mount on your wall. This is an extremely easy project and it can be achieved by mounting a single board onto the wall. Then, to make it challenging, I like to recommend creating a "lip," a strip of raised wood, along the edge of the shelf so that things don't fall off as easily.

Another great project for beginners is the classic birdhouse. It might seem a little old fashioned but birdhouses are incredibly complex projects for how small they are. You need to create a hollow space that can store either a bird or a bird feeder and sometimes both. The best birdhouses even have a cylindrical perch for the birds to stand on, so the woodworker needs to combine boards with dowels to get the project right.

For a more practical project, try a simple bench. You can make a bench with two pieces of wood if you want to strip it down to the bare minimum. You have the piece you sit on and then a thick piece to serve as the legs. This, though, is far more simple than I would recommend. Try instead to make a small sitting bench that uses a piece of wood for each leg and that has supporting pieces to increase the amount of weight it can hold.

These projects might be small but that doesn't mean they don't offer their own challenges. We want to be challenged when we are making something for the purposes of learning. Rising to a challenge is what learning is all about. These projects will quickly raise your skill level so you can start working on the more complex and larger projects found in the latter chapters of this book.

Getting the Proper Lighting For Your Workshop

The last section we need to discuss before moving on is the lighting in your workshop. For some people this will never be a problem that they consider. There's a light in the room, they can see what they need to (or at least then think they can) and that's all there is to it. If you can't see your projects properly, or if you kept casting a shadow over them, then you're going to need to upgrade your lighting.

I recommend that you get shop-specific lighting even if you don't think you have any problems with your current setup.

The main choices for lighting are T8s or LEDs. The T8 is a more traditional light like you'd see in workshops over the years but LED lights have come a long way in the last few years and they are much easier to recommend. LED lights come in just about every shape and size imaginable, they don't get overly hot, they eat up less electricity and they last pretty much forever. Many people recommend the T8s because they have been used traditionally but if technology is changing for the better then we're best suited by adapting with it.

You don't need to place these bulbs in the overhead light sockets. You can use whatever you want in those. What you're going to want to use your LED lights with is a task-oriented lamp or light. If you are going with a light then you're going to want to get a hanging light-rack that you can position yourself. If you're going with a lamp, get one with a long, flexible neck that you can mount on your workbench. Of these two choices the cheapest is the lamp and I also prefer lamps over light-racks because you are able to move them easily to position the light exactly where you need it.

Another reason that a posable lamp is a great choice is the flexibility it allows you as a woodworker. You never know what the next project is going to be or what it will need. You might need light coming from above with this current project, then the following one might require you to work from the bottom, in which case an overhead light-rack will simply not be able to help you. A posable lamp can easily be positioned to throw light upwards from the bottom of a project so that you never have to worry about working blind.

Chapter Summary

- Gearing up can be expensive if you are looking to purchase every piece of equipment possible right away. It is best to purchase high-quality equipment a few pieces at a time. Get only the pieces you need for the majority of your projects and then purchase more as the need arises.
- A woodshop needs to have three key features. The first is enough space to fit your projects, including a door large enough to move the finished product out through. Ventilation (and air conditioning) so that the air quality in the workshop doesn't harm you. The third piece is enough electricity to power all of your gear. Electricity can easily be added to the room while the other two features need to be part of the space itself.
- You can get an energy reader to check how much electricity is being used by your equipment. Remember that even equipment which is turned off, it is using a small amount of electricity when it is plugged into a socket. For this reason, as well

as for reasons of safety, it is a good idea to unplug your equipment when you finish using it.
- It is best to begin woodworking by focusing on smaller projects which you can complete quickly. Many small projects will still offer you the opportunity to experiment with new techniques, tools and tricks and these are fantastic for quickly improving your woodworking skills without the risk of wasting too many materials (which can get expensive fast!).
- Most woodshops will have some natural lighting or some overhead lighting but it often isn't enough. It is a good idea to get hanging or adjustable lights for your key work areas, especially your workbench.

In the next chapter you will learn all about the various tools that we use when woodworking. These range from simple tools like your hammer and your screwdriver to more complicated tools like power drills and electric sanders. You will also learn everything you need to know about the different types of wood available for our projects so that you can pick the one that's right for your next project.

Chapter 2

Wood And Your Essential Tools

Woodworking is an incredibly fun pastime. Without the right tools it would be impossible, or at least incredibly frustrating and likely to hurt. I know I sure wouldn't like to use my hand as a hammer.

Purchasing the essential tools for your projects is important. We'll look at these tools in this chapter. These range from the simplest of our tools, like the above-mentioned hammer, to the most complex, like table saws. We're not going to look at every possible tool that we could buy, as not every tool is essential. It is worth mentioning that sometimes you may want to consider if a more complex or expensive tool is worth the investment. For example, if you think that you are going to be sanding a lot then you may want to consider purchasing an electric sander rather than doing it by hand. It is entirely possible to do it by hand but the amount of time saved with an electric sander can't be discounted. Plus if you're going to be purchasing the electric sander then you won't need to spend as much on buying sandpaper to work by hand.

Considerations like these may result in you spending more money upfront but they have the benefit of saving money in the long run.

The second half of this chapter is going to look at the different types of wood that are available for use in our projects. While every wood is the same, in that they all come from trees, they are also each unique in their own ways and these should be weighed ahead of time when you are planning out your projects. This quick look at the various woods will help ensure you always pick the best species for the job at hand.

Hammer

A hammer is about as straightforward as you can get when it comes to tools. I will assume that you are savvy enough to purchase

nails along with your hammer. I will, however, direct your attention towards the importance of the size of the nails. Nails come in all sorts of different sizes: little nails for small projects; large nails for large projects; nails for connecting pieces of wood together; nails for hanging photos. There are all sorts of nails and you should start with a general nail, a medium size that can work for most projects.

When purchasing a hammer make sure that you pay for quality. It's easy to find hammers for really cheap: usually, an overly cheap price tag is a sign of poor quality. It's always better to spend a little extra money to purchase a tool that's not going to fall apart once you start using it.

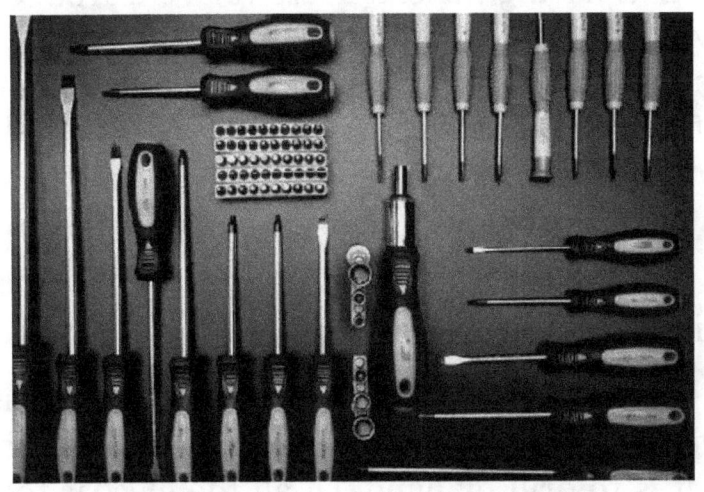

Screwdrivers

You can never have enough screwdrivers. If there is one thing that I've learned from woodworking, it is this. Before I got into woodworking I had one trusty screwdriver that seemed to do the trick for whatever I needed. When I got into woodworking, I discovered that there are all sorts of different screws with different purposes and they each require a screwdriver with a different head. When you're first starting out it can be hard to keep track of them all.

That's why I suggest you drop the money to get yourself a screwdriver set rather than buying them individually.

This will result in you having more screwdrivers than you can use, at least at first. Over time, as you grow more accustomed to working with wood and with screws, you'll find that having the extra screwdrivers around is incredibly helpful. You'll always have the type of head that any individual project calls for and being prepared is always the greatest feeling.

Power Drill

Technically speaking you could go ahead and purchase a plain old drill but you're going to quickly find out how annoying it is to drill by hand. Of all the electric tools you can purchase, a power drill will be the most useful. You'll use it to drill holes for connecting pieces together or for slotting dowels into place. These holes often start small and then work their way up in size and so it isn't enough to buy only the drill.

You are also going to need to purchase a set of drill bits. Depending on the substances you are using, you may find that you need a harder drill than what may normally be required. Since we're working with wood, we should be alright with a normal set. If you are looking to multitask with your power drill and use it on harder materials then you are going to need to invest in diamond-tipped drill bits. These are quite expensive and they can always be purchased at a later date so, for the time being, stick with a good set of drill bits that give you enough variety in size to really be effective.

Saw, Hand

This section of the chapter could rightfully be called the "Saw Section." We could roll these three types of saws into one heading but that wouldn't give them the justice they deserve. The thing with saws is that you actually do want to have multiple saws at your

disposal. With drills, you want one good power drill. With saws, you want a saw that you work with by hand, one that gives you a quick, deep cut and one that lets you take more precise control over the cut.

The hand saw is the non-electric saw that we use. We hold this in our hands by the handle and work it back and forth to cut through our boards. If you are looking to do a quick cut or to simply score a board then your hand saw will be your go-to. A handsaw, depending on what it is made of, can also be good for cutting certain kinds of metal whereas your circular saw or jigsaw could actually chip when trying to cut metal thanks to the speed at which they move. This makes having a handsaw around an incredibly smart idea.

I recommend that you purchase three handsaws. You could stick with one medium sized one but I like to have a small handsaw, a medium handsaw and large handsaw on hand, pardon the pun!, at any given time so that I can match my handsaw to the project.

Saw, Circular

A circular saw is a type of electric saw that uses a circular blade, thus the name. These blades are made for cutting through boards. A table saw also uses a circular blade that comes up from the bottom and you run your boards across it.

A handheld circular saw is quite a bit smaller than a table saw; the smaller size is made attractive by the flexibility it offers as you can reposition a circular saw.

A circular saw should be used to cut boards by first laying the board out either on your workdesk or, more appropriately, by balancing it between two secure surfaces so that you can cut through the board with no concern about striking anything beneath it. A circular saw provides in a much quicker cut than a handsaw does but it offers very little control over the cut itself. A circular saw is best used to create a straight cut (though that doesn't mean it has to be a level cut, so long as it is straight you can use a circular saw to make a diagonal cut). For more control over your cut you should purchase a jigsaw.

If you are looking to save money on saws then the bare minimum you need is a handsaw. If you are looking to purchase one and only one electric saw then I suggest you skip the circular saw for now and purchase our next tool instead.

Saw, Jigsaw

A jigsaw is a type of saw that looks almost like a file. A file, by the way, is one of those all-purpose tools that you may find incredibly useful. The jigsaw's thin, straight, serrated blade moves up and down incredibly quickly to cut through the wood. The thin nature of the blade makes it quite easy to move the jigsaw around corners or to create curved cuts.

The circular saw and even the handsaw are both best used for straight cuts so if you need to cut a curved shape then you have two main options. You can use a straight-cutting saw to make a few different cuts which create the appearance of a curve but with many sharp edges along the bend. You would then take your sandpaper and sand these edges down so that you have your curved cut. Or you could use a jigsaw. The jigsaw will allow you to create the curve in one cut. You'll still need to use your sandpaper to smooth it out afterwards but this would take far less time than it takes to sand out the edges.

Tape Measure

A tape measure is one of those self-explanatory items which is easy to forget when first stocking up your woodshop. Woodworking is an incredibly precise practice. If we're looking to make a chair then we can't simply eyeball the size or length of the legs. If we did then we'd end up with chair legs that are all slightly different sizes and this would lower the quality of the creation as well as its durability.

We use our tape measure to get the exact measurements for each of our pieces. We want to know where to cut, how much we have to sand off and every other possible measurement we can get our hands on.

To do so, we need a way to take these measurements and that's where our tape measures come in. Remember that your tape measure is only half of the job. You'll need a trusty pencil or pen so that you can write down your measurements or mark where on your boards you need to cut them based on the measurements you found with your tape measure.

Chisel & Mallet

A chisel and mallet might be two separate pieces of equipment that are really one tool. They're like hammers and nails, screwdrivers and screws. You have two objects acting as a team that can't be separated. You could use your mallet in place of a hammer if you absolutely can't find your hammer, but I don't recommend it.

Sometimes, we need to chisel out a tiny bit of a project. Or maybe we attached two pieces improperly and we need to separate them so that we can make a more secure attachment. In cases like these, we carefully align our chisel and then strike it a few times with the mallet. This can chip away at the wood, which in turn may result in a lower quality product being produced, so it is incredibly important that you are mindful and considerate when you use your chisel.

Combination Square

A combination square is another measurement tool. It can be used as a ruler for taking small measurements but it is designed in such a way, typically, to include a level. A level is simply a little bubble in a tube. When the level is held, well, level, the bubble will come to rest in the middle of the tube as outlined by two black marks on the tube so that you know your project is balanced.

A combination square will also have an adjustable piece which slides up or down the ruler piece of the combination square. This piece creates a perfect ninety-degree angle to the ruler so that you can measure your corners. It is through the combination of being able to measure corners and check levels that the combination square becomes an essential part of your woodshop.

Clamps

Clamps are simple tools which are used to keep two pieces of wood together. For example, let's say that you want to glue two pieces of wood together. We would apply the glue and then we would attach our clamps to the wood. One part of the clamp would go on the outside of the first piece while the second part of the clamp would attach to the outside of the second piece. We would then tighten up our clamps, if they don't tighten automatically, so that the clamps hold the two pieces together providing the tightest, most secure hold possible, allowing the glue to dry with as little space between the boards as possible.

When purchasing clamps, I recommend that you get half a dozen or even a dozen. You will only need one or two clamps at a time

 when working on smaller projects but as your projects get larger you'll find that you need more clamps to accommodate securing the amount of smaller steps that make up your larger projects. Clamps are rather inexpensive compared to pretty much any other tool that we've looked at so you shouldn't have any problem picking up a handful of them.

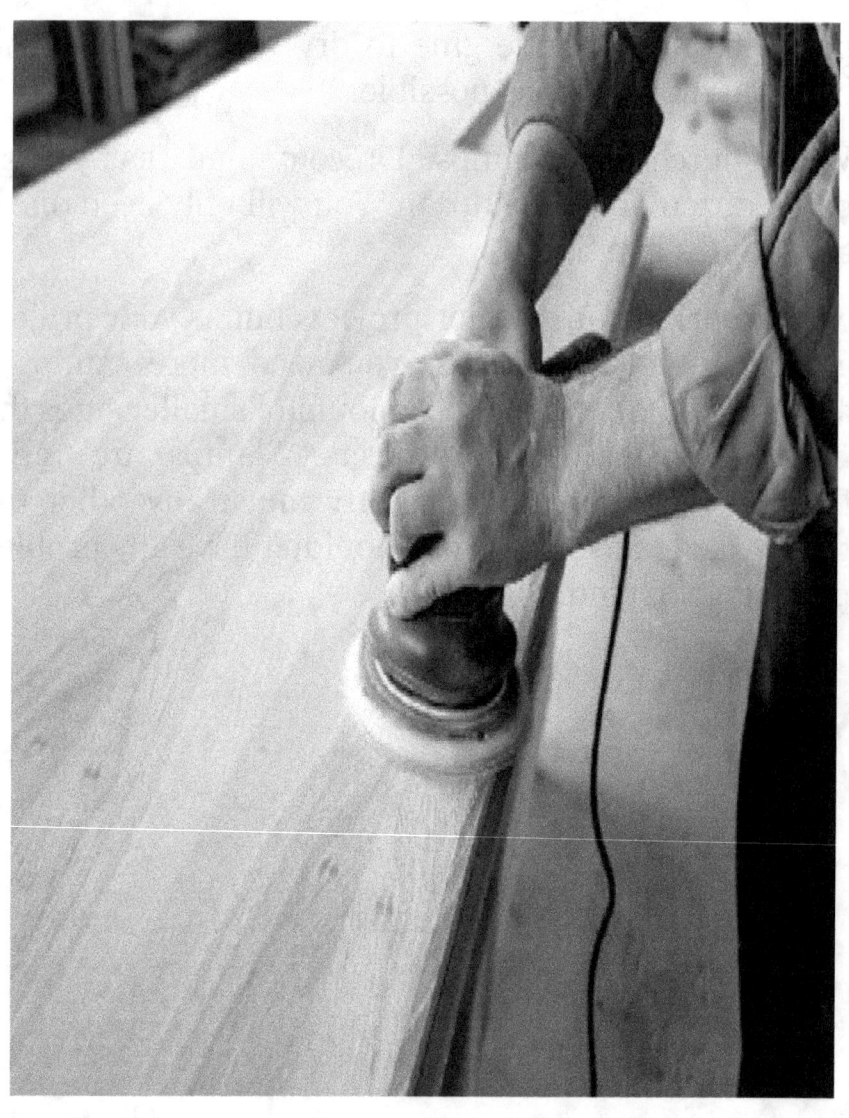

Sander

There are a few different kinds of sanders that are available. You can go entirely non-electric and purchase some sandpaper to work by hand.

Or you can really lean in heavy and spend a ton of money to get a belt sander, though I highly, highly recommend that you don't unless you're looking to make your own knives.

When it comes to woodworking, especially early into your woodworking experience, I believe that the best sander you can go with is a disc sander. This is an electric tool which consists of a spinning head that you attach sandpaper to. The sander spins quickly enough to work the sandpaper over the wood at a rate that is much, much higher than what you can achieve by hand. Doing so results in less time spent sanding, giving you more time to work on the other stages of your project or moving on to the next project.

All About Wood

As everyone is aware, wood comes from trees. Trees themselves are an utterly fascinating topic, as they are truly some of the most interesting biological entities on the planet. Unfortunately, this book isn't about trees and so you'll need to look elsewhere to learn more about them. Woodworkers should know some information about trees before they get started on any projects, though, namely, how they form grains and knots.

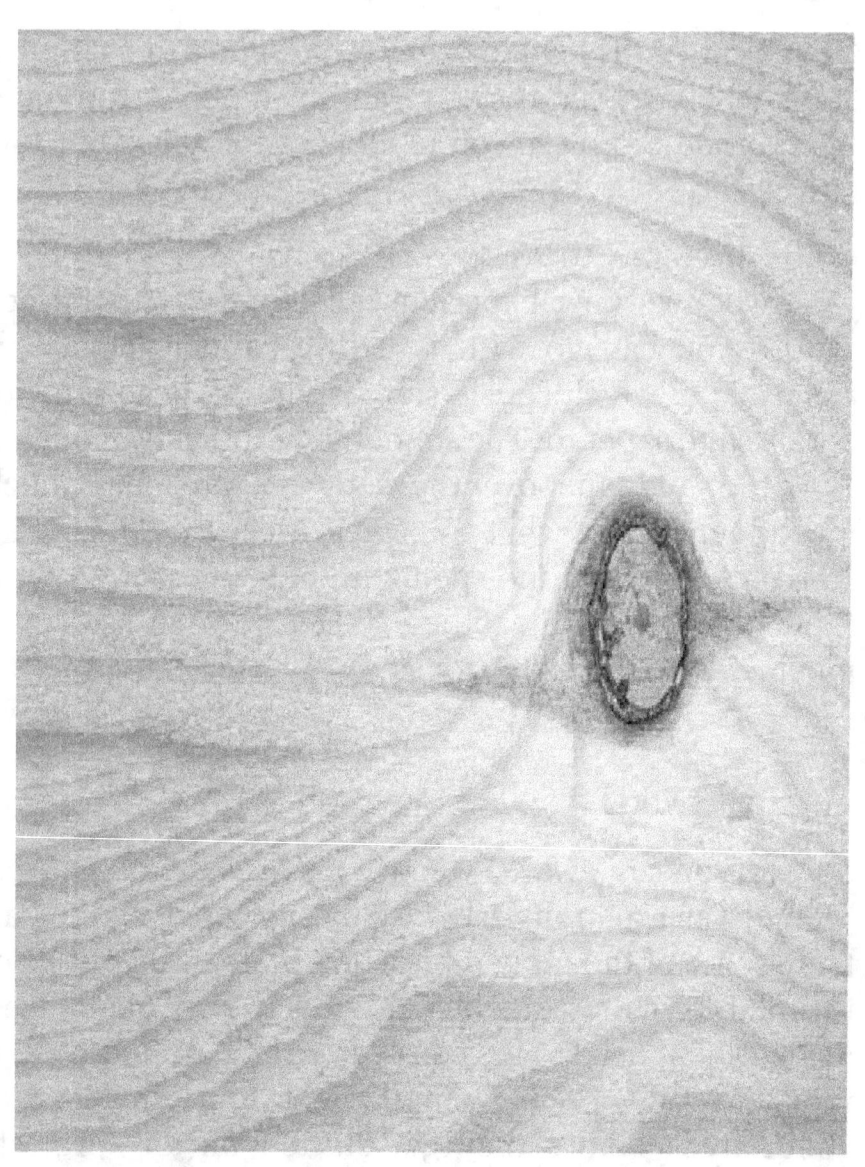

Knots are the easier of the two to explain. If you take a look at a tree, you'll see plenty of branches. But we don't deal with branches when working with wood. Our planks come out of the body of the tree and so the branches have already been removed from the wood at this point.

Knots, however, still had formed on the tree at one point and so we aren't able to completely remove their presence from our boards. Knots form in the spots where the branches once were. These knots are little holes or divots where the branch had been connected to the body. Having one or two knots in a project isn't the worst thing in the world. In fact, they can look quite beautiful. Too many knots reduces the overall quality and durability of a project and so you are best off trying to minimize or even avoid their presence.

The grain of wood is a little bit more complicated. Trees grow a little bit each year. The outermost part of the tree is the bark, which can be thought of as the tree's skin. Underneath the bark are all sorts of tubes that function like our veins do. Nutrients and water move through these veins throughout the whole tree to every branch and leaf. As a tree grows, these veins eventually get stoppered and fall out of use. This isn't a problem for the living tree as it is constantly in the process of growing more veins. When our tree is turned into a plank, all of these veins are still present and they create the grain of the board. Almost every project you work on is best served by working with the grain rather than against it.

There are some projects, however, which specifically call for you to work against the grain and some finishing techniques look best when applied against the grain. Though the finishing coat, at least in this particular matter, is completely up to taste.

Now, let's take a look at our woods themselves.

Ash

Ash is a hardwood. Hardwoods and softwoods aren't so much a description of the wood itself; rather, it tells us whether or not the wood came from a deciduous tree (which loses its leaves in the fall) or a conifer (which typically has needles and keeps them all year). The wood of the ash tree is a lighter color, often white rather than light brown. It has a straight grain and it is quite strong.

Birch

Birch is another hardwood. You can find birch in white or yellow in color. The yellow birch has a light color and a reddish-brown color at the deepest most inner part of the wood whereas the white birch is about the same color as is the wood from a maple tree. They are rated at the same level of hardness as ash wood and thus makes them quite easy to work with.

Cedar

Cedar is a softwood that comes most often in a reddish color. Cedar is rated at the softest level that wood can be. It has a straight grain and is known for having quite the strong smell, which many woodworkers truly enjoy. The first cut of a cedar board is always an aromatic treat. Wood from the cedar tree is commonly used for outdoor projects because it has a resistance to moisture that greatly slows down how quickly the wood rots. All wood rots, however, so you can't prevent it, only slow it.

Cherry

Cherry is a hardwood that is praised for the way it looks once a finish has been applied. Cherry is gorgeous as it ages and so it is a great pick for furniture that will eventually be an antique. Cherry is, however, one of the more expensive woods that you can work with and so beginners who are prone to making mistakes are best off avoiding it. It is a little bit harder than cedar but only to the slightest degree. The wood of the cherry tree has a reddish-brown color, though the outermost pieces of the wood tend to come in white.

Fir

Fir is a softwood that has an extremely noticeable grain. Coming in a reddish color, this wood is quite cheap and so it can be good for beginners looking to practice their woodworking skills. Fir is commonly used by carpenters rather than woodworkers. This is because the grain is quite boring and it really doesn't stain very well. Thanks to the boring grain, even when it does stain it doesn't particularly look that nice.

Mahogany

Mahogany is a hardwood and it is most often selected by woodworkers for their furniture. It had a reddish color, often even a deep red color. The grain on mahogany is most often straight with an interesting texture that takes well to the staining process. It is about as hard as cherry, putting it somewhere in the middle of the difficulty curve. Mahogany can be pretty expensive because there aren't many forests which are growing it in a real, sustainable way.

Maple

Maple is an interesting wood because it can come in both softwood and hardwood varieties. Despite coming in both, it is noted for being one of the toughest, hardest woods out there. Boards made of hardwood maple are quite hard to work with, yet the softwood maple boards can be quite easy, especially when comparing the two. Maple has a straight grain that is quite narrow. Maple is a rather affordable hardwood compared to many of the others that we have looked at.

Oak

Oak is a hardwood that is often selected by woodworkers making furniture. You can get it in white or red types, which are colored according to their names. It isn't quite as hard as hardwood maple but it is pretty close. Many woodworkers like to use white oak as it has a more unique look, which isn't surprising when you consider how many varieties of wood have a reddish or reddish-brown color. White oak has the added benefit of being a good fit for outdoor projects as it is moisture resistant in the same way that cedar is.

Pine

Pine is a softwood that actually comes in quite a few different styles. Regardless of the style, it is commonly chosen by woodworkers making furniture because it is able to stain quite easily. It is also quite a soft wood and this helps it to be incredibly mouldable, so if you wanted to add raised designs to your projects then pine is a great choice. It is also a great choice because it is incredibly inexpensive thanks to its popularity and the fact that it is grown sustainably across the United States.

Poplar

Poplar is a hardwood that is incredibly affordable when compared to the other hardwoods. It is also incredibly soft, being among the softest hardwoods that you can work with. Being soft isn't a bad thing as it can make it easier for beginners to work with the wood. It tends to have a white color with lines of almost green-brown throughout it. It isn't a very pretty looking wood, though, so woodworkers rarely select it. It is more commonly used in carpentry and almost always kept out of sight or painted. There is a trade-off with poplar. It is quite cheap because it is ugly and it is ugly so it isn't as fun to work with.

Redwood

Redwood is a softwood. While redwood can be used for indoor projects it is better suited and more often used for projects that'll be staying outdoors like picnic tables or raised garden beds. This is thanks to the fact that redwood has a natural resistance to the damaging effects of moisture. It's easy to guess what color these boards are considering the name. Redwood isn't the softest of woods but instead fits more into the middle between the softest and the hardest, leaning a little more on the softer side than the hard side.

Teak

Teak is a hardwood that is incredibly resistant to moisture and so, like redwood, is often used for outdoor projects. Redwood is, however, far more often the go-to wood for these projects because it is much less expensive than teak. Teak is actually rather hard to find and so it'll cost you a lot more to purchase. A fairly inexpensive project can grow to be quite costly if you decide to go with teak. It has a gorgeous golden color and a very unique feeling that is hard to beat. If you're looking for a real classy wood, teak is a good choice.

Walnut

Walnut is a hardwood. It is also one of the more solid woods on the list. It's only a fraction of the cost of a board of teak but it is still quite a bit more expensive than your cheaper woods. Walnut is often hard to find and when you do, it is often available in smaller boards. This greatly limits what sorts of projects you can create with it so I would recommend using walnut in conjunction with another wood. For example, if you're making a chair then you can use a more inexpensive wood for the majority of the project then you could use walnut wood for the backrest.

This would be a good fit because walnut looks gorgeous when it has had designs carved into it.

Chapter Summary

- You can't work wood without your woodworking tools. Learning which tools you need and what they do is one of the funnest parts of woodworking.

- A trusty hammer is necessary for every woodworker. It'll let you hammer nails into boards but you'll also find that sometimes you simply need to give a board a few whacks in order to slot it into place or do what you want.
- There are all sorts of different screwdrivers from long ones to short ones and there are tons of different heads that fit into a range of different screws. Get yourself a nice set of screwdrivers so you never have to worry about whether or not you have the right one for the jobs ahead.
- A power drill is used to drill holes into boards. Sometimes, you need to drill a hole in order to get a spot to start cutting a board with a jigsaw; other times you simply need to drill a pilot a hole for a screw or a bolt.
- A handsaw is a saw that you control by hand. It will take more out of you to use a handsaw but you'll have more control over the cut and it's better for cutting through metal than any of the electric ones are.
- A circular saw is an electric saw which is amazing at making straight cuts. You need to be careful using it and you can't control the cut to any degree beyond being straight and so it offers very little flexibility but it is incredibly quick.
- A jigsaw is an electric saw with a single, vertical cutting blade. It is a handheld saw and it offers a lot of flexibility as to the shape of your cuts, allowing for curved cuts easily.

- A tape measure is a must have. Every guide you see for making your own projects will tell you to cut wood to a certain size, and using the tape measure provides that accuracy.
- A chisel and mallet are used for separating pieces of wood that are stuck together or cutting grooves out of the wood.
- A combination square is a ruler, a level and it allows you to measure out perfect 90 degree turns for your corners.
- Clamps are used to hold your wood in place while you cut it or glue it. If the wood shifts around then you're more likely to make a bad cut. Clamps will hold it securely in place so you can make the cleanest cuts and drill the finest holes possible.
- You can use sandpaper by hand. You'll find that an electric sander is faster and less physically demanding.
Sanding is important as we use it to clean up our wood and buff out imperfections that decrease our project's aesthetic value.

- The terms hardwood and softwood are used to describe whether wood comes from deciduous or conifer trees.
- Wood has a grain which is made from all the veins that would deliver water and nutrients throughout the length of the tree while it's growing. Most projects work with the grain but there are many

that specifically work against the grain to great effect.
- Knots occur in wood where branches had once connected to the main body of the tree. Knots are like little holes in the wood. One or two knots are typically fine and can even improve the aesthetics of a piece but too many knots will weaken the durability of a piece.
- Ash is hardwood, light in color and quite strong.

- Birch is hardwood, light in color and about as strong as ash.
- Cedar is softwood with a reddish color, a strong smell and is as soft as wood comes.
- Cherry is hardwood, red in color and pretty soft.
- Fir is softwood with a reddish color, is extremely cheap so is a good fit for beginners.
- Mahogany is hardwood with a deep red color and is pretty high on the difficulty curve due to how hard it is.
- Maple can be softwood or hardwood. Maple boards are quite hard to work.
- Oak is hardwood, often selected for use in making furniture.
- Pine is softwood and often offers a lot of flexibility.
- Poplar is hardwood, quite cheap and soft and therefore a good pick for beginners.
- Redwood is a softwood, red in appearance and well-suited for both indoor and outdoor projects.

- Teak is a hardwood, resistant to moisture and often selected for outdoor projects.
- Walnut is a hardwood that is among the strongest woods mentioned in this book.

In the next chapter you will learn all about the different woodworking techniques that you need to master in order to call yourself a woodworker. These follow the typical flow of a project by looking first at the techniques we use for measuring wood then those we use for cutting wood and drilling holes.

We'll take an in-depth look at our nails, screws and bolts and how we glue wood together to make our connections. Then, we'll create end joints to connect everything and sand our projects.

Chapter 3

Woodworking Techniques

Before we turn our attention over to the various projects that make up the meat of this book, we are going to first speak about some of the important woodworking techniques that we use to bring our creations to life. If you already have experience with woodworking or carpentry then you're likely going to be able to skip to the next chapter without losing much but those that are new to woodworking will want to pay attention.

There are a thousand and one techniques which we could look at if we had the time. To do so would fill up a book ten times larger than the one in your hands and many of these techniques would either be irrelevant for most projects or fall into the classification of 'expert.' There's no point bogging ourselves down with extraneous information. Instead, we will focus on those techniques that are most relevant to our purposes and to the projects in this book.

The techniques that we're looking at will be laid out in a rough approximation of the woodworking process. The middle section is a little blurry, since we might need to use glue on a project instead of nails or screws and so deciding which of these techniques comes first in a global sense of linearity is impossible. The general flow is there.

We'll start with measurements before moving on to cutting and drilling holes. From there we'll look at nails, screws and bolts and follow this with how we glue wood together. We'll then close out the chapter, and thus our imaginary project, by looking at how we can make end joints to connect pieces together and the various techniques for sanding your wood.

Measuring Wood

Measuring your wood is the first step in pretty much every project. If you are making your own projects from the ground up, then technically the first step would be to draft it out and plan it on paper; in that case, measuring the wood would be the second step. We want to make sure that we are making out cuts with as much accuracy as possible and that means measuring as accurately as we can. You might think that every ruler and pencil is the same when it comes to measuring but really it is important that you consider how your measuring tools play a role in that accuracy. We want to ensure we use the right pencil, set a standard with our ruler and double- check our combination squares so that we perfect our measuring technique.

The pencil you use for your measurements might seem like a silly thing to worry about but it absolutely plays a role in how accurate your measurements are. If you've purchased a carpenter's pencil already then take a moment and draw out a line with it.

This line will be thick, actually it'll be about one sixteenth of an inch thick. This is a large enough line that you'll have quite a big difference in the size of your wood depending on which side of the line you make your cut. This isn't too bad for large scale projects that have room for a little bit of variance but for fine projects you'll want a thinner pencil such as one with 5H lead. A 5H pencil makes a line that is noticeably thinner than the carpenter's pencil and this means more accuracy.

There is a trade off. It is much easier to see the marking from a carpenter's pencil. If you're going to be cutting the board with a table

saw then it is typically easier to mark it with the carpenter's pencil so that you can quickly spot where the cut needs to be made. If you are cutting by hand then you increase your accuracy with a 5H pencil. The secret here is to consider what the cuts you will be marking are for and selecting the appropriate pencil based on that. If you are using the thicker pencil then you'll have a higher chance of the measurement being slightly off, so always remember to double- check your measurements after a cut.

When it comes to the ruler that you use there are a thousand options out there. A search for "ruler" on Amazon brings back more than five thousand results, clearly demonstrating how many choices there are.

This isn't a bad thing per se but it does result in a lot of variation between rulers. You might be surprised by this since the whole point of a ruler is to make a measurement and measurements are supposed to be the same but different manufacturing practices result in slightly different rulers. Get yourself a few different rulers and see what happens when you line them up. There is almost always the slightest variation.

The best thing to do is to pick a ruler, at least twelve inches, and stick with it. By settling on a single ruler that you use consistently, you can eliminate any chance of variation between your measurements. This ruler becomes the standard for your work. If the ruler is off slightly, it doesn't matter because all of your measurements with it will be off by the same amount and so your projects will not suffer. This concept should be carried forward with your other measurement tools so that you only ever use the same tape measure for large measurements or the same combination square. By only making measurements with the same tools, you ensure accuracy of the measurements even if they are off from other rulers. It's a bit odd to say but it'll make perfect sense once you get working on your projects. Make sure that you line up your measuring tools with any other measuring devices in the woodshop such as those on your table saw.

Finally, before we get to measuring, you want to make sure that your combination square is actually square. To do this you stick our square up against a straight surface and draw a line.

Then you flip the square over and draw a second line. You can tell that your square is actually square if the two lines are parallel. If they aren't then the combination square either needs to be adjusted or thrown away. Remember to only use the same combination square once you have settled on one that works.

To increase the accuracy of your measurements, always try to measure out from the edge of a board. This creates a reference for you that you can easily return to for later measurements. These will help you to keep your measurements even. Another important technique is to practice your marking. If we mark to the right or the left of the line indicating our measurement then we end up with a measurement that is a millimeter off one way or the other. It is important that we always mark our board as a direct continuation of the line on the ruler we are aiming for. If you are going to be marking more than one part from the same board then try to mark from the same direction. Another useful trick is to keep in mind the front and back of the board as it will end up in the project and to make your markings carefully with this in mind.

Your measurements will get more accurate over time as you practice these techniques. The most important step is the act of ensuring that all of your measurements are made with the same tools. This will create a uniformity in your projects that is the biggest step you can take towards accuracy.

How to Cut Wood

Cutting wood is one of the most common experiences that every woodworker shares. After all, you can't really do much of anything without first shaping and sizing the wood. The first step in the process of cutting is to properly measure and mark the boards. When making these marks you must keep in mind on which side of the mark the cut is supposed to go.

If you're cutting a board from the left then cutting to the left of the mark could cause it to be too short while cutting to the right of the mark may cause it to be too long. Often, we want to cut on the mark itself but this isn't always the case. Sometimes it is better to cut it a little too long and then take off the extra at a later point in time. In fact, I would recommend that beginners cut too long and then sand down the extra millimeters where necessary.

We're going to look at how to cut our wood using three of the most common saws: the jigsaw, the circular saw and the mitre saw.

We could also look at using the table saw but since these are such expensive tools I am working under the assumption that you are starting smaller. Particularly, I am assuming that you have a jigsaw or a circular saw to start out with and that you may be considering expanding your woodshop to include a mitre saw. If you can learn the basics of cutting wood with these three saws then you're going to be pretty much set to use your table saw when you get it.

Before we get to our electric saws, a brief mention on handsaws. These are actually incredibly easy to use. Line your saw up over your measurement marker and start working your hand back and forth. You're going to want to cut with your boards either hanging over the air, such as when it is held up by two workhorses, or you'll want to have a solid surface underneath that you aren't afraid to cut into. Because a handsaw requires you to physically make the action of cutting you can simply stick a cutting board under your measurement marker. Once you hit the cutting board, you stop working the saw and you're good to go. This only really applies to handsaws because you can stop cutting the second you break through whereas an electric saw is going to take another second or two for you to register the end of the cut and in this time the blade can cause unnecessary damage.

Moving on to the jigsaw, we meet my personal favorite saw. The jigsaw is great because it can be used for curved cuts as well as for straight cuts. Many of the saws we use in woodworking are best for straight cuts so having the flexibility that the jigsaw offers is always welcomed. Jigsaws should only be used to make cuts on boards that are hanging over open air. You could try using a cutting board or making the cut on a worktable that you don't mind damaging but even in these cases I would argue that cutting over open air is the better option. We want to make sure that our wood is secure or we're likely to cut it in a mismatched way, curving where we should be straight for example.

When cutting with the jigsaw you must keep in mind that the way the blade functions will have an effect on the cut. The jigsaw's blade points down in a straight piece that has been serrated to be able to cut. The saw brings the sharp edge of the blade up through the wood before it goes back down to then bring the sharp edge up through the wood again. This results in a neat underside. To get a better understanding of this in action, I recommend taking a piece of scrap wood and cutting through it with your jigsaw. Cut through from top to bottom and then go through from bottom to top.

The right side of your jigsaw will move over to the left side when you switch and you can compare the two cuts together to see how the direction of the cut affects the final board. Sometimes you will want the neat side on the final project, so times you won't. Practice with your saw so that you know how the direction of the cut changes the outcome.

 Also practice adjusting the speed of your jigsaw to see the effect it has on the cut.

One last note about jigsaws. Since they are cutting through wood, they kick up a lot of sawdust and wood particles into the air. I always recommend wearing a mask while cutting and either cutting outdoors or in a well ventilated area. You can sometimes get away with making a quick cut in a non-ventilated area depending on the model of jigsaw you have. There are many models on the market which include a little vacuum feature so that the dust is removed from the air as the cut is made. You will need to empty the vacuum after every use and it is easy for this to slip your mind. If you notice that your jigsaw is no longer cleaning the air then stop and check how full it is. Emptying should fix the problem but if it doesn't then you might have a bigger problem that needs to be fixed.

Your circular saw is a better fit for when you need to make a straight line of any real size. It is easier and quicker to run the circular saw down a board than it is to do the same cut with the jigsaw. The blade of the circular saw is much bigger than the jigsaw, though, and so smaller cuts are better left for that tool. These two saws do have more in common than you might at first assume. Despite how it looks, the circular saw actually makes its cut as the blade is rising up and not as it is going down. This means that you can follow, roughly, the same advice about the neat side as you did with the jigsaw.

As with the jigsaw, I recommend that you practice a few cuts from different angles, using different speeds, if the circular saw you've bought is adjustable, and working with the dust removal option. The circular saw is going to have a few more options you should play around with such as the ability to adjust the depth of the cut so that you can work with thicker or thinner boards accordingly.

Cutting with the circular saw is a lot like cutting with the jigsaw in that you'll want to have the board hanging over the open air. In fact, I would go so far as to say that you should pretty much never use your circular saw to make a cut through a board that has a solid surface underneath. This is a recipe for chipping your sawblades and this can get expensive quickly if you aren't careful. There are some accessories and attachments which you can purchase for most circular saws that will help to alter the saw to make it easier to hold or to cut more accurately and are typically optional. Another thing that many circular saws have over the jigsaw is the ability to use different sawblades whereas jigsaws are really designed to use one particular blade. This results in a saw that offers more options for straight cuts but lacks the ability to do decent curves.

After the discussion we had in the previous chapter about cutting along the grain, the biggest thing you need to learn about cutting wood is how to pick the right saw for the right job. Our jigsaw is good for small straight cuts or curved cuts.

Our circular saw is best for straight cuts of any real length (which is also the type of cut that we might turn to a table saw for). What if we want to cut at an angle? We could always measure and mark out our angle and use either a jigsaw or a circular saw to make the cut but cutting at an angle is actually in the wheelhouse of our mitre saw.

We use our mitre saws when we want to make cuts with a particular angle or tilt. The saw itself has more in common with a table saw than a circular saw or a jigsaw because it is stationary. We have to set out our piece of wood at the base of the mitre saw and then use a hand to pull the saw down to make our cut. Because we aren't holding the saw but rather the wood it is actually quite easy to harm yourself with a mitre saw so always approach its use with extreme caution. One way you can reduce the risk of bodily harm is to use the clamps you've purchased to hold the wood in place.

Once you understand when to turn to a particular saw, and have taken the time to practice using each on some scrap wood, you'll see that cutting wood is incredibly easy.

Drilling Holes Properly

Drilling a hole is another common experience that woodworkers need to master. You'll drill holes to put in screws. You'll drill holes to put in bolts. You'll drill holes for hinges.

You'll drill holes simply because you need holes, such as when you need to allow oxygen into a box. Simply put, you'll drill a lot of holes.

Drilling a hole is easy but there are a couple tricks that will make your technique that much easier. It is worth noting that drilling doesn't transition between different materials. You can pretty much punch a small hole into a piece of wood and then go straight to the drill bit that fits the size you are looking for your hole to be. Other materials will require you to start with a small drill bit to create a small hole and then shift up to a larger drill bit, then a larger one, until you get to the intended size.

This is the technique we use when drilling a hole in something like plexiglass. Don't worry, we won't be using this extended technique in the book, I just wanted to ensure that you understand that learning to drill holes into wood doesn't mean you have mastered drilling as a whole.

The first step to drilling a hole in wood is to figure out how thick the wood is so you can select an appropriately sized bit. A shorter bit won't be able to punch through a thick board and it is always best to make your hole in one quick go. The other thing you need to keep in mind before you start drilling is the type of bit you are using. There are all sorts of different bits that create different holes. I recommend getting a kit with several types of bits in them and using them on a piece of scrap wood to see how the holes differ.

If you are following along with a project online or in a book like this then the instructions should tell you what type of bit to use. Practicing will give you the hands-on knowledge you need to be able to select the right bit for projects you've developed yourself.

One last step before you start drilling. You've probably already guessed it, too. Go ahead and mark the location where the hole is to be. Now you can start drilling if you want but it's actually better to reach for your hammer and a nail. Hammer the nail through the marked spot to create a tiny, tiny hole there. In fact, you can reach for your smallest nail for this and you don't need to get all the way through the wood. This action makes it easier to get the drill bit in and to keep it in place.

Place your drill bit onto the marked and indented spot and then set your drill onto a low speed. You're going to want to start low but you can increase the speed as you go. It is always better to start slow and work your way up to fast, as this will create a much cleaner hole and reduce the likelihood of slipping. Put light pressure onto the drill to work it down into and through the wood. Once the hole is made you're going to want to reduce the speed as you start to gently pull the bit out of the hole. Wait until the bit is entirely free from the wood before you turn it off. This last step is one you'll learn quickly. All it takes is one time turning the drill off too early and getting the bit stuck for you to learn.

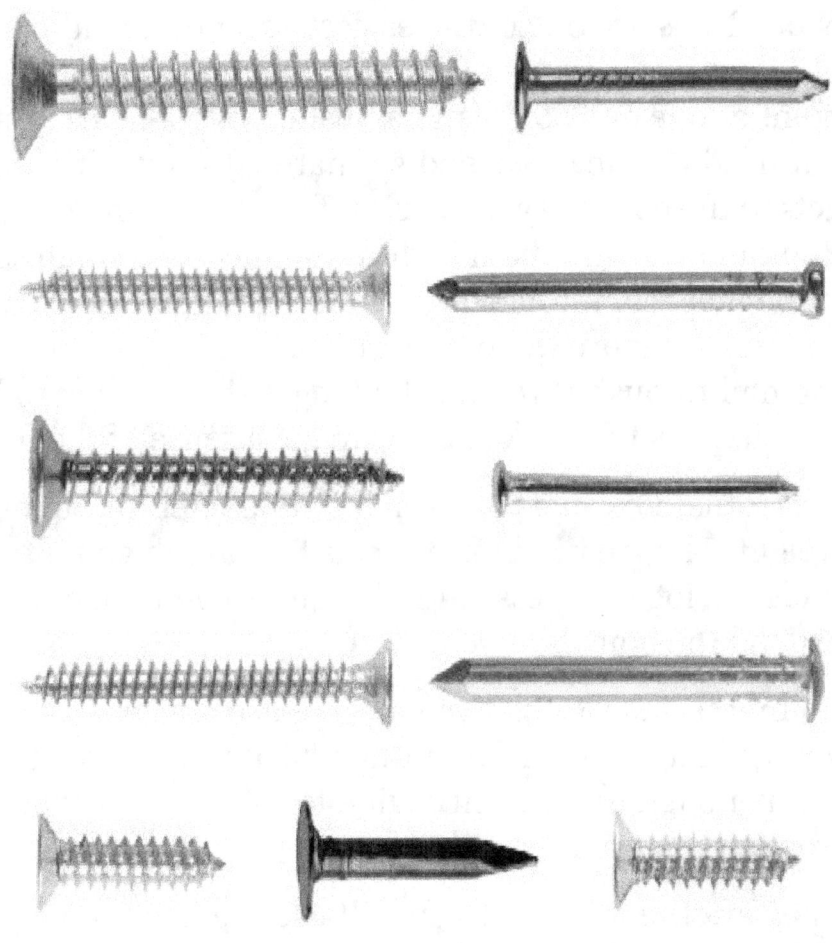

Understandings Nails, Screws and Bolts

We often need to connect two pieces of wood together. We can do that through a fastener like a nail, screw or bolt. The other way we can join two pieces together is with glue so we'll look at that in a moment.

Nails: Nails are one of the easiest-to-understand pieces of woodworking. A nail is a metal tube with a sharp point at one end so it can be pushed into a board and a flat head on the other end so that it stops itself once it gets to the end. They come in different sizes and shapes. You can even find them in different metals, though steel is the most common. Understanding the size of a nail is simple. The more wood or the thicker the wood you need the nail to push through, the longer the nail has to be. For shape, let us look at a few to get a sense of them.

Box Nails: Box nails are small in diameter and light in weight. They're used for projects that aren't going to be under a lot of stress and are quite common for use around the house.

Common Nails: Common nails are used in construction work because they have a thick head that makes them solid enough to push through a lot of different types of wood or material.

They are the nails that you will use the most often and they come in many different sizes.

Corrugated Fasteners: Sometimes called wiggly nails, these are nails that are used for joints where you want them to bend a little rather than hold a strong and stiff position.

Drywall Nails: These nails tend to have an indented head. They are used for holding drywall in place, which requires a lot of strength. If you have a need for a heavy duty nail, it is worth considering the drywall nail.

Finishing Nails: These are light nails that have incredibly small heads so that they don't stand out when used. They're often used for paneling where the presence of a nail head would ruin the aesthetic effect. Another common place you can find finishing nails is the back of an IKEA or otherwise inexpensive bookcase.

Masonry Nails: These are among the strongest and toughest nails because they're made to be used with concrete. Despite needing to be strong to break through the concrete, however, they don't have a lot of holding strength and so should only be used for relatively low-stressed projects.

Roofing Nails: Roofing nails are pretty much common nails with a much larger head that reduces the risk of damage when shingling a roof.

Tacks: Tacks are small, round nails which you can typically put in without the need for a hammer. They are used most often to connect fabric to wood rather than used with wood alone.

Screws & Bolts: Screws are stronger than nails. They also come in many different shapes and sizes. They are defined by the helical threading along their body. This needs to be twisted, or screwed, to get the screw into the wood whereas a nail is hammered with blunt force. Nails are put into a project to hold things in place but they aren't easily removed and so they make a bad fit for anything that might have to be taken apart later. Screws offer more strength plus the ability to remove them easily.

The other defining feature of screws is that their heads are slotted so that a screwdriver can be placed into it. Whereas a nail wants to be flat for the hammer, a screw wants to have a divet that the screwdriver can slip into so that the screw itself can offer support for the screwing or unscrewing of itself. Screws come with all sorts of different divets in their heads for different sized screwdrivers and so you'll want to ensure you have the right screwdriver for the screw on hand. Screws are best used by first drilling a pilot hole into the wood before using the screw.

A bolt is like a screw that isn't sharp at the end. A bolt is placed into a hole and then often a nut and washer is screwed onto the end to create a secure and strong join. They are stronger than screws and therefore stronger than nails.

Carriage Bolts: A carriage bolt has a round head but a square collar. They are tightened by placing a nut on to the end and then using a wrench to work it down the bolt. They are commonly used in furniture but they must have a hole to slot into already.

Hollow Wall Bolts: A hollow wall bolt is used to connect something light, like a picture frame, to a wall that is hollow. The bolt will open up once it gets inside the hollow wall because there is a spring in place that forces it outwards.

Lag Screws: A lag screw has a lot of holding power. They are actually put into place with a wrench rather than a screwdriver. They're most commonly used for framing.

Machine Bolt: A machine bolt is a square or hexagonal bolt that is used with square or hex nuts. The nuts require a wrench to get them into place. They are incredibly strong but mostly used for connecting metal together.

Machine Screw: A machine screw is used to attach two pieces of metal together and so the woodworker won't use them as often.

Masonry Bolt: A masonry bolt comes inside of a plastic sleeve. As you tighten the bolt the sleeve expands outwards to make a tighter hold.

Roundhead Screws: A screw that has an incredibly fine thread so that it can be used with metals.

Sheet Metal Screws: As the name implies, this is another screw we use for metal rather than wood.

Stove Bolts: These bolts typically look like screws and they have a slotted head which can actually be tightened with a screwdriver instead of with a wrench. They are quite strong and offer a lot of holding power.

Wood Screws: Wood screws are pretty much the go to screw for us woodworkers.

Every now and then we'll want to reach for one of our stronger screws and especially for our bolts but if a project simply calls for something to be screwed together then chances are good they're talking about wood screws.

Gluing Together Wood

Our other common way of connecting pieces of wood together is with glue. You might think you understand glue well enough but we'll briefly go over it because it might shock you how much there is to learn about this substance. Right off the bat, did you know that there are many different wood glues?

We're not going to be using the glue you had in your classroom growing up and we sure won't be using glue sticks.

There is yellow exterior glue, which is best for outdoor projects. It tends to be water resistant but it can't withstand constant exposure to moisture. Then you have your white, sometimes yellow, interior glue which doesn't offer any water resistance. Liquid hide glue is used most often for indoor furniture. Polyurethane glue is totally waterproof and so it's what you want to use for long term exposure.

Finally, there is epoxy which is used to fill in holes and gaps and is also waterproof.

Picking the right glue for the job at hand is as simple as considering the needs and placement of the project after it is done being made. If you aren't sure which wood glue you are going to need for a project then you may want to consider buying multiple types. They can last quite a long time and you don't have to worry about them going bad, despite what some myths might state. Keep in mind that different types of glue dry at different rates. It is always best to check the label for dry time, just like you check the label to see if a glue is waterproof or water resistant.

Many people will apply a coat or two of finish to a project before gluing it together. This is perfectly acceptable and can actually save you a lot of time but wood that hasn't been finished is more receptive to glue so it is best to leave a section finish free.

You can do this by simply putting down some masking tape over the part of the board that will be glued. Peel off the tape when you are done finishing and apply the glue with a flux brush. These brushes are great because they let you place an even coat of glue rather than applying a bead and hoping it's enough.

When gluing wood together, we want to ensure that the boards are held together securely. We do this by using our clamps to hold the two pieces nice and snug. We don't want to get glue onto our

clamps, though. The easiest way around this is to use a thin sheet of wax paper over the clamps. Glue might get onto the wax paper and you can throw it out afterwards. Before you apply the clamps, considering rubbing the boards together along the joint they'll connect so that the glue is even more evenly distributed. If you are going to be gluing together multiple boards then you should practice patience. It is always best to focus on one application of glue at a time. Let the first joint dry before you start to add a second one.

If you are looking to attach small pieces onto your wood, anything that's the size of your hand or smaller, then use superglue instead. It'll make it much easier to work with considering the size of the piece in question.

If you are gluing a large piece of wood along the widest part then you'll want to apply your glue a little differently. It's best to use a plastic trowel, one with notches along the end, so that you can spread the glue across the whole of the surface. It can be hard to tell if you are using enough glue in this manner, unfortunately, as there is no easy-to-follow rule of thumb. If you are gluing together two joints then it is pretty easy to figure out if you are using enough. Too little glue will result in next to no glue emerging from between the two boards. Too much glue will result in a solid line of glue emerging. The right amount of glue will create a mixture of the two, where bubbles of glue emerge of differing sizes.

Removing glue is important, too, as woodworkers have a tendency to overuse their glue rather than underuse. This is understandable since it's almost always better to have more than less. Some glue dries clear and you could easily miss a spot where it has been applied. Take a mister and spray a little water onto the wood. The board will take in water but any hidden glue will stand out. You'll want to remove partially dried glue that is sticking out in a bead with a chisel. This is best done half an hour to an hour after it has been applied. Hidden glue on the flat side of a board typically doesn't chisel away so easily. It's easiest to remove this glue with an abrasive pad and a little bit of water. If you let the glue strengthen too much before removal than you'll need a stronger tool such as a paint scraper in order to clear it away.

Following these instructions will ensure that you use the right amount of glue and that you're never left fighting to remove tricky glue that reduces the aesthetic appeal of your project.

How about one more trick before we move on to our end joints? If you ever find yourself with a hole to fill but no epoxy then don't worry. You should have plenty of sawdust around your woodshop. Mix sawdust and wood glue together to make a filler for that hole. This is a quick fix that is great for filling holes on the inside or backside of your projects.

Creating End Joints

Creating the end joints that you'll join together could conceivably, and do often, come before gluing, but this isn't always the case. Understand that a proper picked end joint can make your gluing experience that much easier. There are eight major end joints that we'll look at. These are different shapes and cuts which join together to create a tighter seal between the pieces of your wood so choosing the right one for the right job takes a bit of knowledge.

Straps: The simplest and quickest to install, a strap joint is quite strong but is designed to be hidden from view and you may have issues with screws sticking out from them. They're best used when connecting molding together or parts which won't be resting flat. A wooden strap is cut as wide as possible. Either glue or screw the strap to the piece of wood you are working with. The other half of the strap is then glued onto the strap to create the joint.

Pocket-Hole Screws: Another quick-to-install joint, this one has the benefit of being appropriate for thin boards. It requires a pocket- hole jig, however, and that means more money on equipment. It also will show the screw holes from behind and so it is best for projects which hide the back and take on minimal stress. Use a pocket-hole

jig to drill into the wood at an angle and then add your screws in at that angle.

Splines: This is a strong end joint that can be made hidden or visible, depending on the nature of the project. They need to have an incredibly tight fit or they fail to be effective and while visible splines tend to be stronger they can decrease the aesthetic value of a project. They're best used when you need your joints to be strong. Only use hidden splines where the aesthetics are of extreme importance. Splines are made by cutting out the middle of your two connecting boards so that a third board can be slotted between them. They are then glued or otherwise connected to the third board to create the joint.

Dowels: Dowels are another strong end joint. They're made by drilling holes into one board and adding dowels to another. The dowels slot into the holes, which are filled with glue. This creates a strong connection because it allows you to both glue the ends of the boards together while also gluing the dowels into their holes. You need to use multiple dowels and you need to be extremely mindful of the space between them because you need to perfectly space the holes on the board to match the dowels. These are great choices for when you need lots of strength and you want to hide the joints' connection.

Bevel-Cut Scarf Joint: A bevel is a cut at an angle. If you look at a knife, the bevel is the way that the knife gets thinner as the body approaches the edge. We can use this angle to create a rather simple end joint that is easy to hide within the grain of the wood. This gives us more space upon which to apply glue but it actually doesn't create a very strong connection. It is best for molding rather than larger projects. All you need to do is cut the ends at an angle. A sharper angle results in more surface area for applying glue but it isn't appropriate for every project. Make sure that both ends being connected together are cut at the same angle otherwise they won't join properly.

Mitre-Cut Scarf Joint: A mitre-cut scarf joint is a lot like a bevel cut joint except that the angle it is cut at is horizontal along the board rather than vertical. It creates another large surface area for applying glue and the joint line is easily hidden within the grain. It can be quite difficult to cut both pieces to the identical angle, so you should have plenty of experience with your mitre saw before attempting this end joint. It is good for connecting long pieces of wood together, however, and it offers a stronger connection than the bevel-cut scarf joint does.

Basic Half-Lap Joint: The basic half-lap joint is what is called a face-to-face connection. Basically, take two boards and mark a line down the middle of their end. Cut at that line and remove about an inch from the board from middle to top. The opposite board removes the same length but from middle to bottom. The two boards, if cut to the right size, can then rest their ends over each other. They should look like one board, almost. You have a large, flat surface to apply glue and this creates a strong connection between them. This technique doesn't work for molding or any profiled projects but this is a fantastic joint for pieces that are flat and require lots of strength.

Tabled Lap Joint: The final joint is a more complicated version of the basic half-lap joint. It creates a stronger connection between the two with plenty of surface area for glue. It's also one of the hardest end joints to create, however, and so it will take quite a bit of practice. If you can master this one then you'll have a piece that is worth showing off to people. If you are hiding your joints then don't bother with the tabled lap joint but if you want people to see the joint, and be impressed by it, then this is a good one. This one requires you to cut into the board about an inch from the end to create an almost Lego-like connection between the two boards. The joint connects not at the end of the board but about an inch or two in.

You'll need to perfectly size the cut and even then you'll likely need to trim or sand the ends to get it to work. Once you nail this one, you'll be able to make pretty much any other type of fancy joint you come across.

Properly Sanding Wood

The final technique that we are going to go over is sanding. We sand wood in order to remove marks, reduce the size of a board ever so slightly, make it easier to apply finish and remove unwanted stains. Really, there are any number of reasons that you might want to sand your wood. There are a handful of factors to consider before you start sanding a project. The first of these that we'll discuss is the grit count of the sandpaper you are using. Next we'll briefly discuss fine-sanding. From there we'll look at the three common ways of sanding and finally we'll discuss the removal of sanding dust from the project as it can get in the way of a proper sanding and when we know it is time to stop sanding.

Sandpaper comes in different grit counts. You find these listed as numbers such as #30, #60, #80, #150, #220. These are a few examples, as you can get incredibly fine sandpapers with massive grit counts.

You can also find pretty much everything inbetween, too. You can find a lot of information out there about what grit count is perfect for different types of projects or woods. Honestly, a lot of this information is personal preference rather than any real rule but it does lead to a lot of confusion around which grit count is the best.

We're going to completely toss out the idea of a "best" grit count. Instead we are going to focus on being practical. Since sanding is most often done to remove issues from the board, we want to make sure that the sandpaper we select does so. Therefore, we should start with a sandpaper with a lower number. A lower number has less grit and this means that it is going to be rougher. It will remove more issues but it will also scratch up the surface of the board. This creates quite an ugly look but it will certainly remove any problems such as machine burns or stains.

We don't stop there. Say we begin sanding with a #30 grit sandpaper. We would then move up to a #60 or #80 grit sandpaper. From there we can then jump up to a #150 or a #180 grit paper. With each step up, you'll find that there are less scratches left on the surface of the board and therefore the board begins to look more and more like its natural form. Except that the problem we had with the board was easily removed. If we had started on a larger grit number then we'd find it more difficult to remove the problem because we are sanding away much finer amounts of wood.

If you are in doubt as to which sandpapers to use then start with the lowest grit you can find and purchase a piece of sandpaper with every grit number up until about #180.

You can get sandpaper that goes past #180. There are sandpapers as high as #600 or more! Rarely will you find that you need to use these. Some writing suggests that you should go up this high if you are going to be applying a finish to your work. You may choose to listen to this but really the resulting end product is not going to be noticeably better off for it. A finish tends to create its own surface and so the feel and look of the board is determined by that instead of the sanding. Some finishes, such as those that are oil based, don't create their own surface and so the rough nature of the board will be visible through them. In these cases you may want to sand to a large number but often the roughness of a board brings a certain natural beauty to the end product.

We have three ways that we can sand a project. The first is to use your own hands. We take the sandpaper in our hand, holding onto the back so that we don't injure ourselves, and we work it back and forth over the wood. This actually tends to create a less even result and it should not be used when working on flat surfaces. Hand-sanding is best done when you can fold the sandpaper around an object, such as when sanding the edges of a board to make them less sharp.

Block sanding is a technique we use for basically hand-sanding a flat surface. Instead of using our hand, which applies an uneven amount of pressure to the sandpaper, we instead take a block of wood and use it on the back of the sandpaper so that the pressure is evenly distributed. Cut your sandpaper so that it is large enough to slightly fold around the edges of the block. This will ensure that the entire surface area of the block is being used by the sandpaper.

A more common approach you'll find is to use an electric sander such as your orbit sander. These spin quickly to sand your boards fast. They actually leave less scratches on the board compared to either hand-sanding or block sanding. In order to properly use an electric sander it is important that you understand how to push the sander down into the board. Pushing the sander down will create scratches which then need to be sanded out, ironically. Move the sander over the surface of the wood in such a way as to cover the whole board but without ever forcing it down. An electric sander will also tend to leave a few scratches, though not many. These are best removed by hand using a fine grit sandpaper above that which you had used with the sander. Only use this to quickly remove any scratches. If no scratches were left then you can skip this step.

As you sand, there is going to be plenty of sanding dust that is kicked up. It is fine to leave this while you're using the same sandpaper. For example, if you start with an #80 grit sandpaper then you don't need to worry about the dust while you are continuing work at #80 grit. Once you move up in grit number, you are going to need to remove the sanding dust. This dust will get in the way of your sandpaper and ruin the intended effect. Use a vacuum to suck up the dust between sanding sessions. I recommend a vacuum because it will remove the dust from your workshop without blasting it throughout the air like a brush or a rag does.

Despite what you might think, it can be hard to tell when you should stop sanding. We want to remove flaws and scratches but these can easily escape our notice. At some point we'll find that we are sanding to remove marks that aren't there anymore. It can take a bit of experience to figure out when to stop but there are a couple techniques that woodworkers use to quickly judge. Before you switch to a higher grit count, look at the wood using a light at a low angle to see if you can identify any more marks. The other trick is to lightly wet the wood using a paint thinner and then looking at it from different angles using a low angle light.

This step will make it easier to see if there are any marks being reflected in the light. If there aren't then you've finished your sanding.

Chapter Summary

- Measurements are incredibly important in woodworking. We want our gear to be as accurate as possible. One of the ways we do this is by only having one ruler, one combination square and one tape measure. We check these tools against each other but by always using the same one we can ensure that the measurements are, if not accurate, at least identical in how much they are off.
- Another trick is to use a 5H pencil for your markings as it has a smaller line and thus allows for more accurate measurements.
- Always check that your combination square is actually square before using it. Do this by drawing a line with it, flipping it and drawing a second line. If it is square then the lines will be parallel.
- It is important to cut wood by having it hang over open air. If you cut your wood on a surface then you can damage both your surface and your saw.
- Jigsaws are great because they give you the flexibility to cut curves. They have to be used over open air and it is important to realize the blade cuts from the bottom up.
- A circular saw is used for straight lines. The blade is circular and bigger than a jigsaw but it still cuts at an upward angle.

- It is important to cut along the grain whenever possible.
- Drilling holes is a major step in woodworking. We drill holes for all sorts of reasons. It is typically best to start drilling a hole with a small bit and then to work your way up to larger bits to increase the size of your hole.
- Always remove the drill bill from the hole entirely before turning off the drill.
- There are all sorts of different types of nails, screws and bolts and each have their own purpose and use. Nails are the weakest, screws are your middle option and bolts are what you want to use when you really need some strength.
- Wood glue comes in several different styles but it mostly all goes on the same. You use wood glue to hold two or more pieces of wood together. It is important to learn how to apply enough glue, the signs of too much glue and remember to remove excess glue so it doesn't cause problems for your project down the line.
- Gluing together wood is all fine and dandy but if you want to give your connections even more strength then you need to learn how to create end joints. These are simply ways of joining two ends of wood together. Some are as simple as taking two alternative nicks out of the wood so that you have a larger surface space to apply wood glue and

others are as complicated as drawing holes, fitting dowels and gluing everything together.
- Sanding wood is done to get blemishes and marks out of the wood. We start with a sandpaper that has a low grit count and then work our way up through papers with progressively higher grit counts.
- Sanding by hand is fine for corners and small pieces. Sanding with a brick is better than sanding by hand for larger pieces but the best option is to use an electric sander that'll take the work out of it for you.

In the next chapter you will learn how to make a cabinet with a door on the front that you can either hang on the wall or use loose. We'll also look at how to make your very own workstation so that you can have a space specifically designed for woodworking. This workstation will have a degree of storage but we'll leave its final design open for alterations so we can add more storage, support or whatever we feel we need as we get more deeply involved in our woodshops.

Chapter 4

Storage Projects

We're finally cracking into the projects that the book has to offer. We're going to start with storage projects because you can make these projects to improve your woodshop and increase the amount of space you have for storage and working. I say working because we're going to look at how to make a work desk for your woodshop that is equal parts workstation and storage space.

Surprisingly, the cabinets will be the easiest of the two projects. Despite the fact that the storage space on the table is open and the cabinets are closed there is actually more to juggle when putting together a work table. The combination of storage space and work space can't be beat.

Project #1: A Cabinet

Cabinets can be extremely expensive if you're purchasing them already assembled but making your own is easy and cost effective. In this guide we'll look at how to make cabinets, both the kind that can be hung on a wall and the kind that are entirely self-contained.

These two kinds of cabinet only require a few changes to the building process so you shouldn't have any problems altering your project as needed.

Tools You'll Need:

1. A drill
2. A screwdriver
3. Clamps
4. A hammer
5. A pencil
6. A saw

Materials You'll Need:

1. ¾ inch plywood
2. 1x6 lumber
3. ½ inch plywood
4. Screws
5. Nails
6. Countersunk nails
7. Glue
8. Corner brackets

Instructions

The first step to any project is to plan everything out on paper. You should use your trusty pencil and some paper and sketch out your cabinet beforehand. In fact, you should do this first step on every single project you plan. Even those projects that come with clear instructions and images with dimensions listed will benefit from this practice.

We're going to make our cabinets 34.5 inches tall with a width of 36 inches and a depth of 24 inches. This gives us the three key dimensions necessary for this project because a cabinet is just a box. The height and the depth gives us the dimensions to cut our sideboards and the width and depth gives us the size to cut our bottom and top board. We could technically get away with only using these boards if we wanted though it would be less a cabinet and more a shelf in that case. We'll be using a combination of height and width to figure out our front and back boards in a moment.

We're going to cut the side pieces to length from our ¾ inch plywood. They're 34.5 inch high, 24 inch wide as mentioned.

You can cut both sides at the same time by using your clamps to secure two pieces of plywood together and then making one cut through them. If your plywood is the same size and your measurements are right then a careful cut with your saw will let you get them both at once.

Make sure that those clamps are as tight as can be: any wiggling now will result in an improperly-sized side piece. If you only have one piece of plywood, be extremely careful about the measurements. Before you finish with them, take your clamps and attach both the size pieces together and carefully use a saw - your jigsaw is a good fit for this one - to remove a 3 inch X 5 inch toe-kick from the corner.

Next it's time to cut the bottom. We want this to be 36 inches in length and 24 inches deep. Keep in mind that the way you connect the side pieces will affect the width or length of the piece: diagraming out your project ahead of time is extremely useful. You can use your paper and planning to determine if it is best to attach the side boards to the vertical or the horizontal side of the end piece. Regardless of which you choose, you should consider this long before you glue together any pieces and even before you get to cutting, honestly.

Create panels for the front and the back base by cutting your 1x6 lumber. You want two pieces that are the same width as your bottom piece is. If you are planning to mount this cabinet on the wall then you can completely skip this step. After you've cut the bottom panels go ahead and cut out two pieces that are the same width to serve as the brace panels for the top of the cabinet. Again, if this cabinet is to be mounted then this step can be skipped as well.

We're almost ready to start gluing and nailing our pieces together but we need one more panel. This panel is the front facing panel. These are cut to the size of the boards as they will be seen from the front. This is the part of the cabinet that will be most visible and so it is best to select a lumber which you like the look of. You have two options for the front panel. You can make it 34.5 inches by 36 inches or you can make it 17.25 inch by 18 inches, depending on whether you want one door or two.

Next use your glue to attach your base panels to the bottom board you've cut. You want to make sure that the boards are lined up so that they sit perfectly evenly. One flat face of the base panel should be perfectly aligned with the back of the board while the other is about three inches back from the front. Use your clamps to hold them in place and then after the glue has dried use your drill to make a pilot hole and use countersunk screws to hold it in place.

The sides are then joined to the bottom, first with gluing. Keep in mind that how you connect these joints is up to you but it is easiest to use strap joints. Since you made a slight gap by making sure one of the base panels was three inches out you should be able to fit it securely into the toe-kick that you cut out. Use your clamps to hold things in place while the glue dries.

The back brace panel is then glued on. This is actually pretty easy to do because this part of the cabinet will rest against the wall (as the cabinet should be against a wall even if it isn't being hung) and so you can use a flat surface to make sure it is nice and snug. The front brace panel is added afterwards. This will create a sort of box-like object that is missing the back. We use our hammer and nails to nail the back into place. The various joints are likely not as secure as we want them to be so it is a good idea to use a corner bracket and screws on the inside of the cabinet to hold everything in place.

Before we add the front we might want some shelves. We can measure where we want these shelves to be and then use our pencil to make them. We'll then attach corner brackets so that they sink into one wall and then take a ninety degree turn to point towards the other wall. Screw them into the walls of the cabinet. Cut your shelves to the dimensions inside the cabinet and then place them on top of these corner brackets. You'll need to add screws from the bottom-up into the shelves for extra security.

Finally, use pocket holes and countersunk screws, nails and even some dowels (if you feel the need) to attach the front panels. Make sure to use a hinge along one side (or both if you're adding two panels) to convert them into doors that open and close to complete the project.

Project #2: A Workstation

This next one is more than just a table. It's a workstation. It's going to have most of the features that you'd look for in a fully functional woodworker's workstation. Expect that it's going to be incredibly cost effective and it's going to give you a ton of hands-on experience in the process. In my opinion, that makes it a thousand times more valuable than any workstation you could buy from a store.

Tools You'll Need:

1. A drill
2. A circular saw
3. A hand-held router
4. A mitre saw
5. A sander
6. A screwdriver
7. A wrench
8. A hacksaw
9. A tape measure

Material You'll Need:

1. Two 4x4s
2. Four 2x4s
3. One 49x97 inch piece of ¾ inch MDF
4. One 25x73 inch piece of 1 ½ edge-glued oak
5. One 1/2x1 ½ inch oak board at six feet in length

6. One 1/2x1 1/2 inch oak board at five feet in length
7. One 1/2x1 1/2 inch oak board at two feet in length
8. Two 24 inch pieces of 2x8 oak
9. One 13 inch piece of 2x6 oak
10. 4 3/8 inch threaded rods, 48 inches long
11. 4 3/8 inch threaded rods, 24 inches long
12. 32 3/8 inch dowels
13. 16 3/8 inch nuts
14. 16 3/8 inch washers
15. 30 1 1/2 inch drywall screws
16. 30 s-clips
17. 4 levelers

Instructions

There's a lot of pieces to this project but it can be thought of as three pieces: the base, the top and the vise. The base is made up of the legs and stretches. The top is made up of a shelf to work on. The vise is a specialized section that turns this from a table to a workstation since we'll be able to mount a vise directly onto the workstation to make life easier down the road.

We'll begin by cutting our base to length. For the base we'll be using our two 4x4s and our four 2x4s. Measure out and mark out the legs on the 4x4s. Each 4x4 will give us two of the legs we need. The legs will be 33-5/8 inches long. We want them to be as square as possible and they absolutely must be identical in length. Once you have the legs cut out you can lay them out in front of you to get a sense of the distance there will be between them. The stretchers will be cut to 16 inches for the four short ones and 41 inches for the four longer ones.

Use a router to make the grooves that the threaded rods will use. These grooves should be 3/8 of an inch deep along the long stretches. A side groove of identical depth is worked into the short stretches. It is important that the grooves of each piece be identical to each other. At this point, it is smart to sand the boards if you are planning to. If you are fine with the way they look then you don't need to.

Personally, I have no problem with a workstation that has a bit of a rough look since it's designed for rough work in the first place.

It's time to connect two of the legs together with a short stretcher into what is called a trestle. Stand your legs up on a flat surface and stand up one of the short stretchers between them. Push them together snuggly. We will be drilling holes into them to push the threaded rods through. Mark a position about 8 inches from the end of the legs. This will be where the rod runs through. Drill into it and create a dowel hole through the legs through which you can run your rod. Next you'll want to drill dowel holes into the short stretchers. These holes should line up with the leg holes so that you can use your threaded rods to hold the legs to a short stretcher. We'll be doing this twice as doing it once only gives us one end of the table. It is important to be mindful of the holes you drill for these rods as we'll need to also drill holes for the longer stretchers to connect them shortly.

We'll repeat this hole drilling so that each trestle has a high up stretcher and a lower stretcher. The trestle will look a little like the letter A when all is done.

Drilling the holes through the larger boards can be quite difficult and may take a specialized tool. If you can't drill completely through the large stretchers then it is important to drill as deeply into each as you can so that you can get as much threaded rod as possible from the legs into them.

We assemble the trestle by running the threaded rod through. At this point it is a little bit like putting together building blocks. We have the holes necessary for each piece and we have the rods that will hold them in place. We now need to put them together. Don't be surprised if your threaded rods are longer than you need them to be. We'll slip a washer and a nut onto each of them before we cut them to length with a hacksaw or whatever appropriate cutting tool you have on hand. First build each trestle, which is made up of two legs and two short stretchers. This will give you the ends of the table. You then connect the longer stretchers, to the legs to give yourself the rough approximation of a table. You may need to cut, sand or connect the pieces using additional tools and materials such as nails or screws depending on how well the pieces and holes were cut. It is important that we create a strong table here, otherwise it will be dangerous to work at it.

With the base of the table put together, now is a good time to apply a finish if you are planning to. Otherwise, we'll move on to preparing the top.

We start on the top by first figuring out how we want the layout to be. Do you want the vice to be on the right, left or front? If the front then do you want it to be to the left, middle or right? Decisions like these will allow you to mark out where you'd like screws to go and the like. It's always good to know where all of your holes are going to be long before you get to drilling the first one.

The dimensions of your top are going to mostly be determined before you get to it. After all, it is the dimensions of the base that tell you how large the top has to be. You may want to have a top that hangs over the side to a degree depending on the types of vise you are going to mount into it. This is another step where you should use your pen and paper to get everything figured out before any work actually begins.

We're going to use multiple layers for the top. Our first two layers, aka the bottom layers, are from sheets of MDF and it's best to laminate these. Trim the sheets to the proper size, keeping in mind that it is always better to be a little too big rather than too small: it's simple to remove wood but adding it back takes time and resources. Leave half an inch to an inch extra on each side. Drill holes for the screws that'll connect these two pieces together. You should have already figured out where these need to be located before this step. The screws shouldn't be that long. We want them to dig into the second layer of MDF so that both pieces are held together nice and tight. Before we screw them together we are going to apply glue all along one piece. This needs to be done quickly so it is best to get everything you need gathered up first. Apply the glue across one of the pieces of MDF and then attach the other board. Use clamps and screws now to hold them together.

The edges of the MDF are going to be quite weak. It is best to edge it in order to offer some level of security to the project. Remove the screws from the MDF as it should be securely glued now and trim it down to size since you left it overlong. Use one of your saws to cut edges to the dimensions of the table top. Use glue and your clamps to attach the trim. I find it best to do two sides first, either both the long sides or both the small sides. Once they are in place it is easy to measure the empty space on the sides to get the length you need for the other two sides of edging.

This basically gives us the top of the workstation. You can pretty much copy the steps above to create a bottom storage section that rests on the lower of the stretchers. When doing this it is important to remember to cut out the corners of the MDF to create space for the table legs. Measure the table legs' width and depth and then cut the corners of the MDF accordingly. Due to the difficulty in slotting it in under the table, I find it easiest to cut the MDF in half down the middle and then to reinforce the bottom with a small piece along the center where it has been cut. Otherwise, it is time to work on the vise.

The vise should be mounted to the top of the table. Rather than fixing it to the MDF top, take another piece of MDF and fix the vise to this and then fix this piece of MDF to the first one using your screws. Use your drill to then cover the top of the workstation in bench dog holes. These don't need to go the entire way through the table but you'll want to measure them out so that the distance between them is even.

At this stage we're going to complete our workstation. There is, however, actually quite a bit left that can be done to it. Rather than go over every step of what we could do, this gives us a wonderful opportunity to decide what we want the rest of it to look like and act like. If you are new to woodworking then you probably don't yet know what areas of this skill are the most attractive to you. I recommend leaving your workstation as is for the time being and moving your attention over to other projects.

Build these at your station and see what needs you have. Use these needs to determine how you add- on and expand your workstation. You should consider this product a work-in-progress, as you can continue to add to it for pretty much the rest of your life.

Pay careful attention as you use the workstation to see where it needs extra support. You can always add more screws, bolts and nuts to strengthen it. You can even add reinforcement as necessary. You might be disappointed at first to realize that your workstation isn't everything you thought it would be. After all, you probably didn't expect it to wobble the way it does or that it would drive that splinter into your hand.

These are actually super important opportunities to learn. Fixing that wobble or realizing that you need to sand your station are chances to practice your skills and to go off-book, to decide on an action for yourself and to execute it and see the result. It is through actions like these that the woodworker goes from a beginner to an expert because they offer you a chance to learn without a guiding hand. You learn how to do it for yourself and that is invaluable.

In the next chapter you will learn how to make some awesome and practical projects for use around the home. We'll make a set of gorgeous floating shelves that look much fancier than they actually are.

From there we'll learn how to make a stool for the kitchen so those high up shelves aren't a hassle anymore and then even make our very own pour-over coffee maker so we can get a nice caffeine jolt in the morning.

Chapter 5
Indoor Projects

The next category of projects that we're diving into are those that are meant to be kept indoors. For the most part, this means that you don't have to worry about the moisture resistance of your wood at all, so you're free to choose from any of the types of wood that we looked at in Chapter Two. You can select your desired wood based on how it looks, though it is worth noting that different woods have different challenges and you may want to consider working with an easier wood rather than the most beautiful one.

While woodworking can be used to create beautiful projects and pieces of art that you can hang around the house, I am of the opinion that woodworking really shines when it is used with an eye towards practicality. We want to be able to use the items we've created to improve our lives, even if it is merely in a simple way. That's why I've selected the projects I have. We'll make a two step stool so we never have to struggle to reach the top shelf; we'll make floating shelves to store our goods and we'll even look at how to make our own pour- over coffee maker in order to make our mornings that much more delicious.

Project #3: Floating Shelves

These shelves are a simple design but one that will offer a high level of support compared to other floating shelf designs. They can be used for any number of things such as storing books or spices or family photos. Personally, I have a series of shelves of this kind that start low on the wall and get higher and higher. They're spread all around a couple of the rooms in my house and they serve as walkways for my cats. We experimented with several different designs before finding one that could offer enough support.

Tools You'll Need:

1. A drill (or a jig)
2. A sander
3. A circular saw
4. A stud finder
5. A level
6. A tape measure
7. A screwdriver
8. A hammer
9. Wood glue
10. Clamps
11. A pencil or pen

Material You'll Need:

1. 1x10x8 board
2. Two 2x3x8 boards
3. 4'x4'x1/4" plywood
4. Three 1x4x6' board, same type as your 1x10x8 board

5. 1 ¼" nails

6. 2 ½" pocket hole screws

7. 3 ½" wood screws

Instructions

The reason that these shelves are so strong is due to the support frame that we are going to make for them. The easiest way to make floating shelves is to simply cut a board to the proper size and then

use a bracket to join it to the wall. The result, though, is a shelf that has some small measure of support where it connects to the wall but the vast majority of the shelf is entirely unsupported. We want to ensure that our shelves have as much support as possible. This will take us a little longer but the final result will be worth it.

Before we can work on the frame, we need to first cut the boards to the proper size. Each frame is going to be made of four pieces in order to create a frame that looks like an E. The longest part of the E will be attached to the wall and the three prongs that come out will support our shelf. We can put together three shelves with the supplies we've purchased so this means that we'll be measuring out three long boards and nine short boards.

Use your circular saw to cut your 2x3s to 32 inches to serve as the backbones of the shelves. Next you'll want to use the 2x3s to cut out nine supports that are 7-3/4 inches long. With our raw pieces cut out, we then turn our attention to the process of attaching them together. The best way to do this is to drill in pocket holes that are an inch and a half or so. You can do this with a drill if you are cautious but since we want these holes to be angled you may find it easier to use a jig. Make sure that you use your clamps to keep the supports secured or you'll produce low-quality holes.

We'll use the 2.5 inch pocket hole screws that we purchased to connect the supports to the backbone. Each support should have two holes and therefore use two screws. Line up the end supports so that they are flush with the edge of the backbone. Use your measuring tape to pinpoint the middle of the backbone between the two end supports. It is perfectly fine if the middle support is a little off to either side. As long as it is mostly in the right location then you'll have no problems. It's a smart idea to use your wood glue along with the screws to keep everything in place.

We now have a frame for our shelf but we still want to attach it to the wall. To do this we need to use a stud finder to locate where our studs are. Find your studs and use a pen or pencil to mark them.

Once you know where your studs are, you can then use a level to ensure that you're holding your frame level against the wall. Use the frame, along with your knowledge of where the studs are, to determine where to drill your holes. You want to drill four holes in total into the backbone. Two of them will be between the first and second support and the other two will be between the second and third support. This means that we'll only be using two studs when hanging our shelf. Mark where the holes should be and drill them into the backbone first. Then hold the support against the wall and drill through into the stud to make it easier to attach the screws. Use your 3 ½ inch wood screws to attach the shelf support to the wall.

Once the shelf supports are mounted on the wall you'll find that they don't look like much of anything. They certainly don't look like shelves yet. We could simply lay a piece of wood on top of them and call it a day. These would be shelves but they would stick out like sore thumbs and not be very attractive.

In order to get these looking beautiful we need to start using our plywood.

We'll use the ¼ inch plywood to create a bottom first. We'll cut the plywood to the dimensions of the shelf by measuring the width and depth of the supports and then using our circular saw to easily make the cuts. Use your hammer and nails to nail the plywood onto the bottom of the support.

Nailing from this direction can be rather difficult but it is entirely possible. If you want to make it easier on yourself, then you may want to consider investing in a nailgun.

The bottom piece is not going to be needed for support. It's purpose is purely aesthetic and this is why we can use our plywood for it. Our top piece is the part which everything will rest on and so we'll use our 1x10 board. Use your circular saw to cut the board to 32 inches, or the same length as the backbone.

If you have followed along with the directions then the support should already be 10 inches out from the wall and you should only have to worry about cutting the top to the right length instead of both length and width.

Use your hammer and nails to attach the board to the support. It is also a smart idea to use a liberal amount of wood glue on this step, remembering the techniques for gluing that we discussed in Chapter Three.

We could finish our project here and have a strong shelf but we're going to finish up by adding some trimming. This will hide the inside of the shelves and remove the temptation to try to store something inside like a cubby. If we wanted to make a cubby then we could follow the same steps but instead of attaching plywood at the bottom we would use another 1x10 board.

The support for this board, however, would entirely be due to the nails and so we'd need to create a stronger hold by using some powerful screws.

For the trimming we use a 1x4 board that we cut to 9 ¼ inch. Glue and some nails will allow you to connect this board to the side of the shelf. Do this once for each side. Now we'll add a piece onto the front to hide that cubby but we must keep in mind that we've slightly changed the dimensions by adding the side piece. Using the same type of 1x4 board, we'll want to cut a piece to 33.5 inches in length and then use our glue and nails to stick it onto the front. This closes off the cubby and gives your shelves a full and thick appearance.

At this stage you may want to stain your shelves or paint them. Or you may like them the way they are. It is entirely up to you. If you would like to stain them then stick around for Chapter Seven where we look at the different types of stain available and how we use them.

Project #4: A Stool

Stools are great projects because they require you to really test out your ability to create a solid product. Your floating shelves have to be able to hold up your books or plants or even your cats. A stool needs to be able to hold you up and this means that it has to be a strong and solid piece.

Tools You'll Need:

1. A jigsaw
2. A handsaw
3. A circular saw
4. A router
5. Clamps

6. A dado blade
7. Wood glue
8. A pencil or pen
9. Hammer

Material You'll Need:

1. ¼ inch plywood
2. ¾ inch plywood
3. 12 ⅜ inch dowel
4. Nails

Instructions

Our stool is going to be made out of five key parts. The first part will be the two sides. Despite the fact that there are two of them we're counting them as one part because we are making the same thing twice. The second part is the top step, then the third part is the bottom step. We need to connect all of these pieces together so our fourth part is the dowels that we'll be using to hold it together. The fifth part actually isn't going to be part of the finished product but rather we'll be using a piece of plywood to create a template for the sides so that we already know they're done correctly before we even cut them.

The first thing we're going to do is cut all of our boards into pieces that are pretty much the size we want. Normally I would say more or less but when it comes to these rough cuts it is best that they are more rather than less. Cut the sides by cutting your ¾ inch plywood into two pieces that are roughly ½ inch by 6 inch by 10 inch. Next cut the top step out of the ¾ inch plywood so that it is ½ inch by 10 inch. The bottom step is cut from the same ¾ inch plywood to a size of ½ inch by 6 inch by 10 inch. The dowels are cut to ½ inch by 10 inch. Finally, cut your template board out of the ¼ inch plywood to a size of ½ inch by 10 inch. These are far from our final pieces but you could start to assemble a truly crude stool out of them.

Next up is to use the dado blades to cut a groove into the wood. This is a type of end joint that will be particularly effective for supporting the weight of a person. We set up our blades so that they cut about three quarters of an inch wide. We want the cut to also be at a depth of about 3/8 of an inch. We'll make two grooves like this on each side board. One groove at the top for the top step and one groove ten inches from the bottom for the bottom step.

Now it's time to make our template for our sides. We want a bit of an odd shape for these sides. We're going to cut out half an oval from the bottom-middle. Since we cut from the middle it will have the effect of creating a front leg and a back leg. From the front leg, take a steep angle up towards the top. We want it to have this angle so that it'll be easy to step up onto the top step from the bottom step. If we made the side straight then we'd have an angle that makes using the stool more like using a tiny ladder and it would prove to be quite uncomfortable. The back left will take a little inward curve as it moves towards the top, just enough to be noticeable but this has the effect of strengthening our step. Nailing this part can be quite difficult but that's why we practice first on paper and then with a template long before we cut the wood. Use your jigsaw to cut out the template and carefully sand it so that it is as smooth as possible. We'll be using the template to make our cuts.

We want to be extremely careful when cutting the sides and so we won't clamp the template onto them quite yet.

Instead, take your template and place it on the side board. Use a pencil or pen to trace the template onto the board and then set the template to the side. Remember that you are creating a right side and a left side and so you have to flip the template over between sides, otherwise you would end up with two right sides. Use your jigsaw to cut the side boards but don't follow the traced line perfectly. It's best to consider this a rough cut and instead cut it a little wide so that you can still see the traced line you will have mostly followed.

Take your template and place it back onto one of the sides. Use your clamps to really hold it in place. The clamps aren't going to offer enough hold on their own, however, so first clamp it and then use your hammer to nail the template to the side. Use a router to trim the edges down so that they are perfectly aligned to the template. Now remove the nails and do the same thing with the other side. This step gives us our perfect precision.

Next we want to make a mock-up of the stool before we glue, nail or screw anything. Use your clamps on either side of the stool and slot the steps in where they are supposed to go. Leave your bottom step hanging out over the sides, as we want this step to be forward when it is done so that it is easier to step onto. The top step should be flush with the back.

If you cut everything to the sizes above then the top step is going to hang over the front a bit. We're going to be cutting these steps in a moment but to do so we need to keep them at the same angle as the front of the stool. We do this by simply tracing along the side of the steps where they meet the sides. Once you have traced the angle of cut onto the boards you can create a bevel cut at this exact angle. Now everything is cut and you are ready to start assembling.

The dadoes and rabbets that you made earlier offer a lot of surface space for your wood glue. Apply your glue and stick everything together. Use your clamps to hold everything in place. Let it dry, remembering to remove any excess glue beforehand otherwise you'll need to chisel it off. You can remove the clamps once the glue has hardened. Take your drill and drill through the sides into the top step twice and into the bottom step three times. These holes should be about two inches deep. Use a 3/8 inch bit so your holes are the same size as your dowels. Stick a dowel into each hole to make sure that it fits. Take the dowels out, add a dab of wood glue, stick them back in and then cut them with your hacksaw so that they are flush with the sides. Sand the end of the dowel to make it smooth.

Project #5: A Pour-Over Coffee Maker

Pour-over coffee has become incredibly popular in the last few years and why not? That's delicious coffee! It can get rather expensive to stop at the coffee shop and purchase one each morning. It's also pretty expensive to purchase your own pour-over coffee maker. Did you know that you can make your own coffee maker at a fraction of the cost? You don't even need to worry about eating up electricity. You can do the whole thing with wood alone!

Tools You'll Need:

1. A mitre saw
2. A drill
3. A wrench
4. 2 ½ inch hole saw
5. A funnel

Material You'll Need:

1. 1x6 board, about three feet
2. Two ⅓ x 2 inch hanger bolts
3. Two ¼ x ½ inch well nuts
4. Two wood screws
5. Two ¼ inch hex nut
6. Two ¼ inch flange nuts

Instructions

We need to get all of our wood ready. The approach to this easy- to-make project will be like our step stool in that we'll get everything cut to size and ready and then simply put it all together like a jigsaw puzzle. The first thing we want to do is cut our 1x6 board. We need three different pieces from this board. The first is 11 ½ inches and it will serve as the backbone to the project. The second cut is 8 inches and it'll be our bottom. The last cut is the top piece which we'll cut to 6 inches. Finish up these cuts by sanding the edges to remove any roughness but be careful not to reduce the dimensions in doing so.

The way the coffee maker works is by holding a funnel in place at the top through which the coffee can slowly drip. This means that

we'll need to drill a hole into our top piece for the funnel to rest in. We want this hole to be as close to the middle of the board as possible. We'll be using hanger bolts on the back of the project so it's important to leave an inch and a half from the back of the board so that they'll fit. Next flip this piece onto its side so that you can drill pilot holes into the thin backside. These are where the hanger bolts will go. We're doing two of them, each one about an inch from the side. It's a good idea to clamp the board beforehand so it doesn't move. Screw the hanger bolts into place by first attaching a hex nut and a flange nut to the end. Make sure that they are held together securely so that they don't come apart when using your wrench to twist the bolts into place.

We'll finish prepping the pieces by using our drill to put four holes into the back piece. These will be used to readjust the size of the coffee maker based on the size of the cup we're using since on-the- go cups have a tendency to be taller than at-home mugs. The first set of holes should be about an inch from the sides and roughly two inches from the top. These holes should be in a straight line with each other on a horizontal plain. The second set of holes should be about four inches from the top, directly below the other two so that they are in line with each other horizontally and in line with the previous holes vertically.

Now, let's put it all together. Use your clamps to hold the bottom piece to the back and take your drill to make pilot holes for your screws. Keep these holes in a vertical line with the previous holes. Screw the back piece to the bottom piece. Take your top piece and slip it into one of the sets of holes you made previously by simply slotting the hanger bolts through. Use a flange nut and tighten it to keep the top piece from falling. If you need to readjust the size of the coffee maker then all you need to do is take off the flange nut, move the top piece to the other set of holes and add the top piece again.

All that is left is to stick your funnel in the hole, grab your coffee and your mug and start pouring. Oh, and enjoy your pour-over coffee as the fruit of your labor.

In the next chapter you will learn how to make a handful of different outdoor projects from vertical planters to raised garden beds and even a sack toss board game so you can maximize the use of your outdoor space and entertain your friends and family.

Chapter 6

Outdoor Projects

Woodworking projects aren't only for your kitchen and living room. There are many amazing projects you can work on to create all sorts of awesome and unique products for your yard. The range of things you can make is actually impressive. There are chairs and tables, stools and planters, walkways and arbors. There are decorations and games, toys and even tools. The possibilities are truly nearly limitless.

In this chapter we're going to again focus on practical projects. We'll learn how to make a sack toss board game to entertain our friends and family during cookouts. We're going to make raised garden bed planters to give personality to our yards and also improve our gardens. Plus, we'll make a vertical planter to grow plants when space is limited. Don't worry if you don't have the greenest of thumbs in the garden: there are thousands of other projects that you can make with these skills to improve the beauty of your lawn and increase the comfort of your life.

Project #6: A Sack Toss Board

Sack toss is a simple but fun game that many people first play in elementary school. It's a great excuse to get the kids out of the

house and it can make entertaining guests that much easier while everyone is waiting for the meat to finish grilling on the BBQ. Making a sack toss board is easy, though you'll need to provide your own sacks to toss or you can do like me and buy some tennis balls: great for replacing sacks and entertaining your dog!

Tools You'll Need:

1. A circular saw
2. Clamps
3. A jigsaw
4. A drill
5. A compass
6. A screwdriver
7. A pencil or pen
8. A tape measure

Material You'll Need:

1. Four 1x4 boards
2. Two 2 feet x 4 feet pieces of plywood
3. Two bolts
4. Twenty screws
5. Two nuts

Instructions

We're going to begin by first cutting our wood to size. We'll take the 1x4 boards and cut them into six different pieces. The first two pieces will be 48 inches long. These will serve as the sides of the project.

Next we'll cut two pieces to 22 ½ inches long to serve as the front and the back of the project. The last two pieces are the legs and these we want at 15 inches. We'll actually be reducing the size of the legs shortly but, as you've hopefully caught on, it is always better to go a little bit larger and reduce in size slowly than it is to cut too small to begin with.

Guess what? We're already quite a ways through the project! There's still plenty left to do but the cutting of the boards gives us

everything we need for the frame and after that it's pretty much home free. So let's finish up that frame. Connect your four frame pieces together using two screws for each connection. Remember to drill pilot holes for your screws before you add them. Connecting these four boards together should take eight screws, with two at each corner. Make sure that the edges of your boards are flush with one another for the best results. This gives us the frame, so now we need a top to toss our sacks through.

We're using our plywood as the top of the game board, so we'll cut holes out of it through which we toss the sacks. There are a lot of options at this stage. You could go classic with a single hole at the top or you could add multiple holes. If you're adding multiple holes then you could keep them the same size and in a straight line or you could switch up their locations for some fun or you could even make some holes larger and some holes smaller and assign point values to each of them. It is entirely up to you how you design your board but for the purposes of teaching we will assume that you're going with a classic, single hole design.

For a classic design you'll want the hole to be in the top middle of the board. You can pinpoint this location by using your measuring tape to measure nine inches from the top. From there use your measuring tape to go twelve inches from either of the sides and then use your pencil to mark the location. This is the center of the hole we'll be cutting. Next use your compass to draw a hole that is about six inches in diameter or so. Again, you can make it larger or smaller depending on your needs. Younger children will have an easier time with a larger hole but adults will enjoy the challenge of a smaller one. Once you have your hole drawn, take your drill and a small bit and drill a pilot hole. This pilot hole is simply so you can fit your jigsaw into the board without any issues. If the hole isn't big enough for the jigsaw blade then switch to a slightly larger bit. Use the jigsaw to cut out the circle by following along your drawing.

Now it's time to attach the front piece to the frame. Use your clamps to hold the plywood onto the frame. Drill pilot holes into the corners.

We're going to use two screws for each corner but we'll use one on each of the sides so the top right corner will have one screw that sinks into the right side board and one that sinks into the top board. These don't need to be perfectly measured so eyeball about an inch from the top and an inch from the side. Remember that the screws that go into the side boards are those measured from the top and the screws in the top are measured in from the side.

We'll use a total of eight screws, so eight pilot holes, to connect the corners of the board to the frame. At this point you should have four screws left over. You could remove the clamps if they're in your way but if they aren't then go ahead and drill a pilot hole in the center of the top, the center of the bottom and the center of each side. Use your remaining screws to finish up with the top.

These extra four screws are for added security, it is really the screws in the corners that are going to be doing most of the work. If you want an even more secure top board, you could apply wood glue along the edges before you begin adding screws but really this step would add time to the building and the benefit would be barely noticeable.

That finishes off the top of the project, now we attach the legs. We've cut them to a rough size but we'll want to size them even further: they haven't been cut to the proper size yet. We'll give them a rounded shape on the end that connects to the frame. We do this by finding the middle of the board and then measuring an inch and three quarters down from the end. Use your pencil to mark a spot and then use your compass to make a half circle towards the end of the board. Take your jigsaw and cut off the corners of the board by following this tracing. You don't need to drill a pilot hole this time since you can start directly from the edge. Repeat this for both legs.

Flip your frame over so you can get inside of it. We're going to attach the legs. Pick a spot on the side about an inch from the top. We're connecting the legs to the frame by the rounded end, remember. Use your clamps to hold the legs in place, taking extra caution to ensure that they are parallel to one another. Use your drill to drill through both of the side of the frame and the leg that you

have clamped in place. Before you do so, take another moment to ensure that you will be drilling through the center of the leg on the rounded side. It will still work if you are a bit off from the center but you will need to then be even more cautious to ensure that the second leg is off-center to the same degree. Once the holes have been drilled use your nuts and bolts to hold it in place. Repeat for the second leg. You should be able to swing the legs in an arc.

At this point we're almost finished but our legs are still a tad too large. Find yourself something that will let you lift the sack toss board up about a foot off the ground. Keep in mind that we only want to lift up the top end, as the bottom end will remain on the ground. Once you have the top end lifted, swing the legs out and off the side of your work table. You'll want to do each leg separately as it is important to keep the leg snug against the side of the table. If you've followed along with the sizes then at this elevation the legs will dangle past the top of the table and you'll be able to use the table as a ruler to mark a straight line with your pencil on the bottom of the legs. If done properly, the line you draw will be the same on both legs. Use your circular saw to cut the legs along this line. What you've done is determine the right size for the legs to be able to elevate the board for play.

With that, you are done, except that your sack toss board is going to look pretty plain. You're going to need paint to add the finishing touches that'll make it stand out.

You can paint it all one color or use multiple colors. You can add words of encouragement or point values for the holes. It's your game, so paint it how you feel it looks best.

Project #7: A Raised Garden Bed Planter

A raised garden bed planter is one of the most useful and productive projects that you could make. If you are into gardening at all then you should be using raised beds: they let you plant earlier in the season, reduce the amount of issues related to weeds and pests and they allow you to increase your yield per square foot. If you aren't into growing your own fruits and vegetables then they can be used to create flower beds and really add a lot of beauty to your property.

Plus they're easy to make and you can offer your know-how to friends and family to make their lives easier. I highly recommend learning how to make these amazing planters.

Tools You'll Need:

1. A hammer
2. A circular saw
3. Moisture resistant wood glue

Material You'll Need:

1. Four 2x12 planks
2. Twelve pieces of rebar, 2 feet
3. Newspaper
4. Soil
5. Nails

Instructions

Raised garden beds are so easy to make that we don't even need to cut the boards if we can find them at the right size. We are, however, going to work under the assumption that we'll have to cut our boards to size. One of the cool things, though, is that we can make a raised garden bed that's about any size. For our purposes, we'll be making an eight foot by four foot box but this is almost entirely adjustable.

Why only "almost?" Well, for that we need to take a quick second to discuss how a raised garden bed is used. Once you understand this, you'll be able to make your raised garden beds at any size you desire.

These beds are used to grow plants. They're really amazing because they vastly reduce the amount of weeds and pests you deal with but this doesn't mean that they allow you to neglect the plants growing in them. They still need to be watered and looked after, checked for pests and signs of disease. Because of this we want to be able to examine any of the plants we grow in the raised bed. The hardest plants to check are those in the middle and so we never want to make a raised bed that is more than four feet in width. Anything more than this and it will be hard to reach the plants in the middle and they'll end up neglected. We can, however, make a raised bed that is less than four feet wide. We can also make a raised bed that is any length we want. It could be forty feet long and work perfectly fine so long as it isn't more than four feet wide.

Keep this width rule in mind when making your raised beds. We're going to take set dimensions in this build but you can change those as you desire so long as you remember this rule and keep it rectangular. Technically, you don't need to keep it rectangular but different shapes and sizes offer different challenges and they'll require you to alter your build from this one accordingly. This guide will work for rectangles and squares.

 Cut two boards to eight feet and two boards to four feet. This is the only project in the book that doesn't need to be put together in the woodshop. In fact, it is a thousand times easier to build this one outside where it is going to be used. Lay your boards down in a rectangle so that their corners are touching. Lift up one of the eight foot boards. Hold this board in place by grabbing a heavy object, getting a friend or family member to hold it in place or by ramming two pieces of rebar into the ground near each end. We're going to be using the rebar to offer support anyway so this can get us started. To get the rebar in the ground simply position it in the ground and give it a few blasts with your hammer to secure it.

Lift up one of the four foot long boards. If you've already started with the rebar then you might as well use one or two pieces to hold it into place. A raised garden bed exerts a lot of pressure against the wood so the rebar is necessary. You could technically get away with using the rebar as the only supporting mechanism but I suggest attaching the boards together with nails and wood glue. Once you've connected the end to the side move on to the next side and repeat the process. Finish up with the last end.

You now have a square box on your lawn. This is the raised bed, really, but it doesn't have enough support. Use the rest of your rebar to hold it all together. Once you have the rebar evenly distributed and everything feels secure, you might notice that the rebar really stands out, quite literally, from the rest of the project.

Use your hammer to drive the rebar further into the ground so that it no longer stands taller than the wood planks do.

Take your newspaper and lay it out over the bottom of the raised bed. Use your garden hose or a bucket of water to wet it. Then fill up the raised bed with soil. This is the moment of truth. If the bed has been properly supported then you won't have any problems. If there isn't enough support then you'll see the sides start to bulge out and then break. This happens because gravity is pulling the soil down; it wants to spill outward and down in every direction but the boards are holding it in place. With enough strength, they'll hold it but if they aren't properly supported then the weight of the soil will break them.

Project #8: A Vertical Planter Stand

Sometimes, there isn't enough space to be able to set up a raised bed.

For example, what if you're living in an apartment and all the space you have is on your balcony? When space is an issue then it's time to start thinking vertically. That's where this particular planter stand comes in. Because we're making a planter stand, that doesn't necessarily mean that's what you need to use it for: you can use this stand for any number of things. You could hang decorations off it, use it to dry your clothes, use it as a vertical sack toss board even.

The sky's your limit.

Tools You'll Need:

1. A jig (Kreg)
2. A drill
3. A circular saw
4. Clamps

Material You'll Need:

1. Two 2x2 furring strips, 8 feet
2. 1xs8 board, 8 feet
3. 2 ½ inch Kreg screw
4. 1 ¼ inch Kreg screw
5. Three flower pots
6. Wall planter hooks

Instructions

We start by cutting our wood to size. Cut the 2x2s into six pieces. Two pieces are 13 inches long, two are 65 inches long and two are 12 inches long. We'll also cut the 1x8 board into 7 pieces that are each 13 inches long. Use your circular saw for these cuts.

We want to make pocket holes for our screws. We do this with our jig. Each of the 13 inch pieces we cut from the 1x8 board are going to get two pocket holes at one end and two pocket holes at the other end. We want these to be three quarters of an inch deep. After that we'll stick with our jig but set it to 1.5 inches deep to add two pocket holes to the ends of the two 13 inch pieces we made. That means that each of the 13 inch pieces will have four pocket holes in total. We're going to add two pocket holes at the ends of the 65 inch pieces but only to one end, not to both.

If you're going to stain or paint your wood then now is the best time to do so. After we put it together you can still paint it but it's

going to be harder to get into the cracks and corners. Once you're satisfied with the results then we'll start sticking everything together.

Use two appropriately sized screws to attach the 13 inch pieces to the top of the 65 inch pieces. From there we'll move onto the 1x8 pieces and attach these to the frame we've just made. It's important to keep the backs of these pieces aligned with the back of the frame. Go through and add all seven of these pieces to the frame. After all seven are attached then use your clamps to hold the boards while you attach the two 12 inch pieces of 2x2 to the bottom of the frame. These will serve as the legs of the stand and so we want to attach them at a perpendicular angle rather than keeping them in line with the rest.

At this point you now have a stand. It isn't a planter yet but you should be able to stand it up on its feet without it wobbling and falling over. We finish up the project by using our drill to make pilot holes and then screwing in our wall planter hooks. These look like tiny basketball hoops but they're designed for plant pots to rest in. Of course, to fully make use of this creation you're going to need some plant pots to rest in it but I'll leave those up to you.

In the next chapter you will learn all about the different types of wood finish we can use to make our projects really stand out. These finishes are used to change the way a project looks but also they offer protection against the elements or even UV rays. We'll look at how to apply stains and finishes and then explore the different types.

Chapter 7
Applying Finishes

It's appropriate that the last step of our projects tends to be applying a finish. This isn't always the case, as sometimes it is easiest to apply a finish before putting pieces together, but it is the case enough of the time to warrant this chapter coming last.

Wood finishes come in two types. Surface finishes are easy to apply and they tend to leave the wood looking natural, if slightly exaggerated. They're called surface finishes because they are applied over the surface of the wood. Penetrating finishes are also applied over the surface of the wood but these finishes penetrate into the wood to improve the longevity of the wood at the cost of a natural appearance. Both types of finish have their uses and they both have beautiful aesthetic value to offer to your projects.

In this chapter we'll look at how to apply these finishes and then we'll talk about the different finishes we can use from dyes to paints, from oils to lacquers.

Finishing Wood

There are two stages to finishing wood but they aren't always the same. You'll always need to start by preparing the wood but after

that you'll move into staining or finishing depending on what type of finish you are using. Technically speaking, staining wood is a form of applying a finish but it's a specific form which will have its own, mostly similar, steps to be followed. We always begin by preparing the wood so we'll start there.

In order to properly finish the wood, we want to have first sanded it. Wood naturally has a lot of scratches and nicks, dents and scuffs. These occur as the wood is shaped, transported, sold and then worked on. This gives plenty of time and opportunity for the wood to get marked up and there really isn't a whole lot that can be done about that. These marks will reduce the wood's aesthetic charm and a finish will only highlight these marks. The first thing we do is use a sandpaper with a high grit count to remove these marks. We tend to start with a grit count around 120 and move up to 180.

You may not have to move up from 120, as it will often be enough to do the job; check after you finish sanding to see if the board needs more or not. If you need to, move up the head to 180 and if this hasn't done the job then move up again to 220.

At this stage, you should wipe away all of the dust kicked up from sanding and inspect your wood. We do this stage between each progressively finer sandpaper we use but it is especially important that we clean the wood before we apply the finish as anything left on the wood is going to cause the coat of finish to go on unevenly and this will reduce the aesthetic value of the piece as much as leaving marks and nicks would have, thus defeating the purpose. Once you are satisfied with the wood and you've cleaned it up, you can apply the finish.

Whether you're staining the wood or applying another finish is going to determine which path you need to take from here. We're going to first discuss how to stain the wood as this is the quicker method of the two. Afterwards we'll talk about applying our other finishes and then we'll close out the chapter with a look at what those finishes are like.

When you've selected your stain, you might not actually like the color. It is best to test out a little bit of the stain on the wood first to ensure that it is the color you want it to be. If possible, do this on a piece of scrap wood from the same board you started with.

You apply the test stain the same way you would regular stain. Open the can of wood stain and give it a little stir. Avoid shaking the can. Use a paint brush and brush a little stain on the wood. If the color is what you want, continue to the next step; otherwise, get yourself a different color of wood stain and repeat this step.

You can use a paint brush or a clean rag to apply your stain to the wood. You'll want to make sure that you let the stain drip back into the can for a moment before applying it, that way you don't let it drip all over your project. A rag will let you apply stain at a faster rate than a brush but you'll have less control over it and therefore it'll be harder to apply evenly. It is best to start with a small area to begin with. If you have a small piece that you are going to apply stain to, start there and pause. Take it slow and see how long it takes for the stain to dry. You want to work the stain into the wood and wipe away any excess stain. Watching it dry will give you a sense of how long it takes to apply a coat and to tell if you've used enough. Brush on the stain, wipe away the excess. Repeat this until the entire project is covered.

You might find that the stain isn't dark enough. You don't need to run out and purchase a darker stain if this is the case, simply wait until after the stain has dried and then apply another coat to darken it up. It is important that you always allow the stain to dry before adding another coat. To apply more than one layer of stain at a time would change the color of the stain in an unpredictable way.

It may look good but chances are it will look uneven, splotchy and low- quality. Otherwise, that's all there is to staining.

Applying finish is a longer process because it necessitates applying more than one coat. Start by choosing the finish you want. There are many options to choose from and we'll be getting to these in a few minutes.

We prepared the wood by first sanding it as mentioned above but we'll be repeating this in a few moments anyway. First, apply your finish the same way you applied your stain. Stir the stain but don't shake it, use a paint brush, let the brush drip back into the can before you start applying. You'll work the finish over and into the wood with a paint brush rather than a rag, as a rag only works with stains.

After the coat of finish dries, you'll find that the grain of the wood has expanded and that the soft surface you had after sanding is now rough again. This can't be helped. Take out a really fine sandpaper like a 280 grit count piece and quickly sand the piece. This should be an extremely quick sanding since there isn't much to be worked away.

Remember to clean away any dust that's left over as leaving it will cause issues.

Once you've sanded the paper it's time to apply a second coat of finish. Do this exactly like you did the first, using your brush and being careful to keep the application nice and even. After this coat is done then you'll move on to sanding the piece a second time, again with the 280 grit count paper. Then you'll apply your finish again. Then sand it again. Then apply your finish again. Then sand it again. You'll keep repeating this until you've applied five or six coats of finish. We apply so much finish because it doesn't only improve the look of the piece, it actually helps to protect it from moisture and decay, so we want to ensure that there is plenty of finish applied to our pieces.

Dye

Dye is a finish which you select when you want your finish to be the same color as the surface it is being applied to. You select your dye like you would a paint for a touch up: by carefully testing colors to find which is the match. You can find dyes in both water- and oil-based varieties. Dyes help to protect against decay but they don't offer much in the terms of moisture protection and so they are best used for indoors projects.

French Polish

French polish is a finishing technique that was developed in the 1800s in France.

It is made by mixing shellac with alcohol to create an extremely glossy appearance. Out of all of the wood finishes there are, French polish is the glossiest. It is an oil-based application as you first apply oil to a rubbing pad and then use this pad to apply the polish.

Lacquer

Lacquer are incredibly thin finishes. They can be applied with a spray rather than with a brush and they dry incredibly fast. They work so well in this manner because the solvent in the spray

evaporates and leaves only the lacquer itself on the wood. Lacquers are a deep penetrating finish which gives a glossy appearance but more importantly really helps to highlight the beauty of the wood grain. If you like a natural appearance with a bit of gloss then lacquer is the way to go.

Oil

While some finishes we've discussed come in oil varieties, this doesn't tell you that much about what it means to be an oil finish. An oil finish helps to keep your wood protected from moisture and rot and so they're great fits for indoor or outdoor projects. Your wood naturally has oils in it and these help to keep it flexible and tough. As the oils dry out, it becomes easier for the wood to crack and break. An oil finish actually replaces these natural oils and creates a seal to help trap the oil in the wood so that it lasts longer.

Shellac

Shellac is a finish that is based on wax. In fact, it is actually taken from the secretion of certain insects. These insects feed on trees and then their waxy secretions are collected and mixed with alcohol to create a great consistency for application. To be clear, this has happened in order to make shellac so you aren't mixing the alcohol into the finish. If you were to do this then you would have made French polish. Shellac comes in many different colors, has a glossy appearance and it is incredibly easy to apply and is well liked for how quickly it dries.

Stain

Stain helps to improve the natural color of wood. It will darken it in a really rich way, though you can purchase stains in different colors. It's best to select a wood stain that is darker than the wood you are trying to stain, so if you're looking to end with a brighter color then you'll want to go with a different type of finish. Wood stains really make the grain of the wood stand out but they don't offer any protection to the wood the way most finishes do. For this reason, it's best to use a coat of stain and follow it with a coat of finish, usually something clear and water-based.

Varnish

Varnish is made by mixing resin, a typically alcohol-based solvent and oil together. A varnish goes on clear and makes a good pairing with wood stain. It isn't selected to change the appearance of the wood but rather to protect it from decay and the harmful effects of the ultraviolet rays of the sun. This makes varnish a good choice for projects that'll be sitting outside or near windows. Varnish is slow to dry and it should be the last layer of finish applied to a project, otherwise you are kneecapping how much it can protect your wood.

Water-Based

A water-based finish tends to have a less overpowering smell compared to an oil-based finish. They are also thinner, quicker to dry and typically quite clear compared to oil-based finishes. Water-based finishes bring less attention to themselves for this reason and so they are best for when you really want the natural beauty of the wood to be the center of attention. They don't help to protect the wood to nearly the same degree as an oil-based finish does, especially because of how quickly they dry out. They are easy to apply, though, and this makes them a great choice for those experimenting with finishes for the first time.

Chapter Summary

- Wood finishes come in two types: surface finishes, which are applied over the surface, and penetrating finishes, which are applied over the surface then penetrate down into the board.
- Wood finishes are mostly applied the same way, except if the finish is a form of wood stain. Wood stain gets applied in its own way.
- Before applying any finish you must first sand the wood. Start with a grit count around 120 and then move your way up to a higher grit count until all blemishes in the wood are gone.
- Make sure that there is no sanding dust left on the piece when you apply the coat of finish or it will cause blotchy sections.
- Apply stain with either a paint brush or a rag. A rag makes the job quicker but it reduces our ability to distribute stain evenly.
- If your stain isn't dark enough then you can apply another coat after it has dried.
- Applying another other coat of finish requires us to sand the wood first and then apply the finish with a paint brush. After the finish has dried we

sand the wood again because the grain will have poked out. We then apply another coat, sand the wood and apply a third coat. We typically end up applying five or six coats of finish.
- A wood stain will stain the color of the wood but it won't offer protection to the wood. Most types of finish will offer some level of protection.

Final Words

We've made it to the end of our time together and I hope this is the beginning of your journey through woodworking. This is one of those skills that you'll find to be invaluable. Just think: you want a new bookcase? Make it yourself. Do you need a new work desk? Make it yourself. Want a new deck for the yard? Make it yourself.

With this skill, you can make pretty much anything wooden that you'd ever want. Plus you can do it at a fraction of the cost of buying new or paying someone else to make it for you. That's some amazing savings.

Remember that every single project you work on teaches you how to be a better woodworker. Even easy projects are an opportunity to learn. You can experiment with using different techniques, different types of wood, different tools. You can always switch up any step in a project to see how a slight change alters the flow of the project. This will let you find those steps that you can take short cuts on or those tools which you love using. Maybe you don't like using a circular saw but instead like to do your cuts with a jigsaw, that's perfectly fine and entirely up to you.

No matter where you go from here, make sure that you don't give up on this skill. Practice making chairs or tables or planters or kitchen appliances.

Find those projects which you consider to be the most fun and really dedicate yourself to improving your skills and you'll find that it rewards you both in the new products you make but also in the act of doing itself. For me, the best part of woodworking is the actual working of the wood, the smell of a fresh cut or the look of a freshly stained piece or when you're able to measure out a board just right to get all your pieces cut and thereby save another board for later use. These are the best parts for me: find that part you love the most and then hold it dear to your heart.

In this book, we briefly looked at how to get started woodworking and what tools we need. There are always more tools to purchase, if you so desire, just like there are a dozen different types of wood to play around with. We looked at several different techniques but we've barely even scratched the surface of what's out there to learn. We made storage projects, indoor projects and outdoors projects but even these are merely a drop in the ocean of possibility that now resides within your hands thanks to the time you've put in woodworking.

So get out there and dive into that ocean to make the coolest, most unique, most you projects that you can. Then put them out into the world. Show them off to friends and family.

Gift them to friends and family. Sell them at craft shows and cultivate a name for yourself so people will bring commissions to you specifically.

When you do that, you'll find that this skill is fun and lucrative, too.

No matter what you do, don't forget to have fun and enjoy the smell of a freshly cut board.

www.ingramcontent.com/pod-product-compliance
Lightning Source LLC
Chambersburg PA
CBHW070107120526
44588CB00032B/1371